B10

THE VIRGINIA BISHOP
A Yankee Hero of the Confederacy

THE RIGHT REVEREND DOCTOR JOHN JOHNS
Fourth Bishop of Virginia

The Virginia Bishop

A Yankee Hero of the Confederacy

By

JOHN SUMNER WOOD

GARRETT & MASSIE, Incorporated
Richmond, Virginia
1961

2147

DEDICATED TO—

OCTAVIA

MARY AND PEGGY

CONTENTS

Foreward.. xi

Preface.. xiii

Chapter I Who Was John Johns.................... 1

Chapter II John Johns in Maryland................. 11

Chapter III Bishop Johns in Virginia............... 27

Chapter IV Bishop Johns, President
College of William and Mary.................. 81

Chapter V Bishop Johns—Bishop Meade.............115

Chapter VI The Virginia Bishop—An Appraisal.......135

Appendix.......................................161

Bibliography....................................175

Index..177

ILLUSTRATIONS

Page

The Right Reverend Doctor John Johns .... Frontispiece

Interesting Old Views of College of William and Mary   4a

Ann Van Dyke Johns 20a

The Three Johns Brothers 20b

Amstel House, New Castle, Del. 36a

Transportation Prior to 1859 .... 36b

Old Court House, New Castle, Del. 36c

Some Christian Leaders 36d

Civil War! 52a

Bombardment of Fort Sumter 52b

Confederate Leaders 52c

Castle Thunder 52d

Sherman's Brigade at Battle of Sudley Church 68a

Battle of Malvern Hill 68b

Portrait of The Rev. John Johns 84a

Portrait of Rev. John Johns 84b

Four Presidents 100a

Harper's Ferry in 1859 .... 100b

The Right Reverend William Meade, D.D. 116a

Three Outstanding Christian Generals 116b

The Four Bishops of Virginia 132a

Immanuel Church, New Castle, Del. 132b

Kensey Johns, II 148a

Susannah Galloway Johns 148b

Chief Justice Kensey Johns, III 164a

Holographic Will of Bishop John Johns 164b

FOREWORD

A rewarding experience is assured to the reader of this impressive book. It will undoubtedly change many previously held concepts, too, concerning the significant and often unheralded contribution of the church during the formative years of our nation, particularly of the Commonwealth of Virginia. Bishop Johns, affectionately known as "The Virginia Bishop," emerges from the pen of the talented author John Sumner Wood as a true man of God.

Possessing a delightful sense of humor and accepting success with abject humility, the good Bishop was compassionate, talented, and blessed with sympathetic understanding of the weaknesses and strengths of his fellow human beings. His was not an ivory tower religion but the daily symbolizing and the applying of Christ's teachings.

The Virginia Bishop's sterling character and his dedication to God and country faithfully represented and patriotically interpreted the political and social mores of his time. Bishop Johns' honored place in history, not only in the religious field but in all activities of human endeavor, is richly deserved.

A. C. WEDEMEYER
General, U. S. Army (Ret.)

March 31, 1961

PREFACE

This is not a book on religion, although the ministry presents a dramatic challenge to any young man to whom the Call may come! Bishop John Johns and General Robert E. Lee—you name a few more—were among the giants of their time in America.

The rugged individualists pictured among these pages are silent sentinels in ink coming forward to greet you as you, by the magic wand of imagination, wander back in time to catch a glimpse of The Virginia Bishop of 1796 to 1876..

I am not interested in one John Johns merely because he happened to have been a spectacular and vigorous Episcopal Bishop. What I want this biography to illustrate, through the medium of Bishop Johns, is that mankind's greatest national force is the intangible Christian output of its dedicated spiritual leaders.

Socialism, the ownership of all property by the state, is materialism and no more. Democracy gives mankind the freedom to correct the abuses of capitalism by evolution and also to enjoy the blessings of Christ-like thoughts, ideals and goals in work, play, love and worship.

JOHN SUMNER WOOD

Woodbyrne
Darnestown—Seneca Road
Germantown, Maryland

CHAPTER

I

Who Was John Johns?

John Johns of Delaware, the Yankee Bishop of the Confederacy, was one of the great orators of his time, one of the four foremost Presidents of the College of William and Mary, and by all standards one of the most Christian gentlemen of our nation. What's more—manly armies bowed with him in prayer; and saw him, almost seventy years of age, ride like a raider and risk his life to reach the battlefields' wounded and dying. To the simple folk he gave this dignified title—"the honorable post of private soldier."

This biography has been written primarily because the Rev. Dr. Randolph H. McKim, D.D., LL.D., writing about 1916 for the *History of the Theological Seminary In Virginia,* regretted that "in undertaking to give a sketch of Bishop John Johns of Virginia . . . we are seriously embarrassed by the fact that no life of this eloquent and distinguished prelate has ever been published. . . ."

The Rt. Rev. John Johns, D.D., LL.D., of Delaware, between 1849 and 1854, was President of the College of William and Mary, and between 1842 and 1876, Assistant Bishop and Bishop of the Protestant Episcopal Church of all Virginia. Bishop Johns, a non-Virginian, baptized and confirmed Jefferson Davis in 1862, and confirmed General Robert E. Lee in 1853. Swift in his race and mighty in his results, he, a physically powerful,

1

brave, and humble servant of God, for sixty years studied, taught, preached, and lived for Christ and His Cross.

Of course this biography is not a detective story but it does have a touch of mystery, and even a skeleton. Yes, a skeleton that once had a graceful figure, lovely complexion, flowing hair, sparkling blue eyes and pretty lips. She bore, and her dainty feet rocked the cradle of Johns' descendants, and Dr. McKim probably had her in mind when he chose the words—"seriously embarrassed." The skeleton was Bishop Johns' beautiful sister, Henrietta.

Bishop Johns' mother, Ann Van Dyke Johns, daughter of Governor Nicholas and Elizabeth (Nixon) Van Dyke, of Delaware, "was a great beauty. General George Washington and General Lafayette were both at her wedding," on April 30, 1784, at Amstel House, Newcastle, Delaware, "and General Washington" (an authority on American beauties from Massachusetts to Georgia) "told the groom that he should be a very happy man, as he had married one of the most beautiful women in the country."

I make no attempt to give a chronological story of the life of John Johns. This biography is different: it presents a series of word pictures of different phases of the lifetime services of Bishop Johns in a young and vigorous nation, for which the illustrations in this book add an historic panorama of human interest. There will be some repetition after contrast to convince you that John Johns is *The Virginia Bishop*.

Piecing together the crystal fragments of Bishop Johns' way of life really is a pleasant privilege but this mosaic would be easier for me if Johns had had some weaknesses, some flaws, some prejudices, or had become involved in some bitter North-South controversy of his time, or left some enemy, or adverse critic, instead of having easily made, and generously served, so many friends, and led such a blameless life.

You know of the wild controversies that raged all around John Johns from the calmness of George Washington's Farewell Address to an infant nation of sixteen states in 1796, to the angry election of our nineteenth President Hayes in 1876, from the War of 1812, from the rumblings of secession and rebellion of the Hartford Convention, from the bursting of the sin of slavery over the admission of Florida and Maine, from the Mexican War of aggression, the bitterness over tariff, the tensions of 1850, the days of "Bleeding Kansas," and on through the War To Cleanse The Union, to the limp and prostrate end of our "tragic era" of Reconstruction, yet the eye of the storm is a quiet place, and peace and calm did follow The Virginia Bishop all the days of his life. I am presenting a man's life. I am attempting to reconstruct, against the background of our nation's history, a genius whose life was devoted to the service of God above self.

The transition from the Established Church of England to the Protestant Episcopal Church of a new and free nation, followed by the impact of Methodism and other attackers, was a harsh blow for our Church to absorb. Even Chief Justice John Marshall said that "the Episcopal Church was so hopelessly prostrate in Virginia that it would be wrong to encourage young men to enter the

ministry," but John Marshall was an Unitarian, and
never an Episcopalian. Those grave years presented a
soul-searching challenge to brave and educated young
men such as John Johns of Delaware.

John Johns, born in 1796, entered Princeton at age
sixteen and was graduated in the Class of 1815. He had
had two years at the Theological Seminary of Princeton
when the sacred Call to duty carried him into the Episcopal ministry. Ordained deacon in Philadelphia at age
twenty-three he immediately went, not home to Delaware,
but to Frederick, Maryland, and it was during that
1819-1829 period that the Rev. John Johns became one
of "a little band of men whose force of divine purpose
gave to the Episcopal Church of America a strength
greater" than that of hooks of steel. The loss of hope
on the part of John Marshall, and many others of his
age, had an electrifying effect on the more vigorous
youth of America. Jesus needed men who were giants,
to stand up and be counted; and up stood young John
Johns of Newcastle, Delaware.

When the Episcopal Church was weak, John Johns
was one of its most devoted Christian defenders. About
1837 a new church was built for him in Baltimore. At
age thirty-two, and again in 1838, he missed by three
votes becoming Bishop of Maryland. He was a minister's
minister, a man's man, so eloquent, so manly in his
devotion to God, that at the Virginia Convention at
Staunton in 1842, he, a non-Virginian, whose Quaker
relatives in Maryland had freed their slaves in 1807,
was elected on the first ballot an Assistant Bishop by a
vote of forty-three out of forty-nine, and consecrated

Interesting Old Views of College of William and Mary

©*Harper and Brothers, Used by Permission.*
From a lithograph of a drawing by Thomas C. Millington, about 1840. Many variations of this illustration are known. Very probably as the College appeared in Bishop John's presidency.

©*Harper and Brothers, Used by Permission.*
Probably the work of a modern artist. The period is after 1733, when the President's House (at right) was completed.

View, from the southwest, of the main College building as rebuilt after the fire of 1859, but before the fire of September 1862.

in St. Paul's Church, Richmond, in 1842. He was the
first Bishop consecrated in Virginia. John Johns ap-
prenticed himself to the service of God at a time when
one branch of Christ's family of denominations needed
him the most, wanted him the most, and afforded him
the opportunity of rendering his most devoted service.

"Bishop Meade was a Virginian of the Virginians
and dwelt among his own people." The point is that
there always had been a strong sectional tendency in
Virginia to save most high offices for gentlefolk, "upper-
class" Virginians, so it was a singular honor for John
Johns of Delaware to have been chosen Bishop of Virginia. Bishops Moore and Meade imported some highly
educated northern clergymen who "were not native but
adopted sons of the old state," outsiders who helped
rescue the tottering Church from the reactionary grasp
of "the ruling classes of Virginians." An evangelical
revival, humanized under Bishop Johns, returned an
aristocratic Church to its fundamental precepts.

Bishop Johns was the great evangelical prelate of
the Church in Virginia and the most typical domestic
missionary Bishop in America. No Bishop of Virginia ever
came more scholastically prepared and rendered more
humble service to all the people of the Protestant Episcopal Church than did John Johns of Delaware. In the
words of the hymn of his long-time friend, Francis Scott
Key, Bishop Johns truthfully could testify: "Lord, with
Glowing Heart I'd Praise Thee."

Sprinkled throughout the 1842-1876 period of the
Virginia Episcopal Church, and tucked away in everyone's memory of the 1824-1876 Seminary In Virginia,

were the constructive acts, the good deeds, and kind words of Bishop Johns. To young ministerial students he gave practical, positive advice. He would say, "Young gentlemen, be much with men." He never neglected his duty to preach to the Negroes. Others remembered him as a "witty and good Bishop." He planned carefully; he performed with perfection; he led with grace; he drew out of others their very best performances, all with a minimum of effort on his part; so the results of his labor were many blended patterns of human harmony. He, though Bishop, lived in such daily Spartan simplicity, that people, students, and teachers walked with him through the struggles, and the chaos, and the confusion of his period not sensing that they were being guided and calmly led by one of them, who was their Bishop Johns.

His twenty-three years prior to 1842 were devoted to the duties of being a Rector in Maryland, not far from where his emigrant Quaker ancestor, Richard Johns, had settled about 1660 at "The Cliffs" in Calvert County, Maryland. Suddenly, in 1834, Columbia, Princeton and University State of New York each conferred an honorary D.D. on him. He, in 1842, was selected by an austere, aristocratic Bishop of Virginia to be his Assistant Bishop. From 1842 to 1862 he devoted himself to knowing his Diocese and by so doing he learned how to carry out many fundamental social reforms when his time came to become Bishop in 1862. Actually, for fifty-seven years he remained thoughtful and simple in the Holy Ministry; and, like the mighty oaks that grew on The Hill, he never lost out to the years as they came and went. He gave no thought to his own importance. Bishop Johns, a genial humorist, was tender but strong; at proper times serious but not sanctimonious; overpowering by his modest thoughtfulness, characteristically kind and true, and both a learned scholar and a princely Christian gentleman amidst all kinds of emotional environments.

Who was John Johns? In Virginia, Bishop Madison for a time saved the Episcopal Church from oblivion and Bishop Moore did his best, as did Bishop Meade but Meade tended toward showing favoritism for the "gentlefolk" aristocracy of Virginia. The evidence proves beyond all doubt that Bishop Johns, and not Bishop Meade, is The Virginia Bishop. Bishop Johns left his family background and wealth in Delaware and went to Maryland, and to Virginia, as a bride with naught save the Bible and a cheerful, confident faith. He completely remolded his whole environment. By his self-made Christlike character he reformed the whole Episcopal Church of Virginia. By his prayer and physical might he dragged the bleeding Church from the battlefields of a political-economic Civil War and nursed it back to health and to renewed vigor, and, in his time as prelate, presided over a happy family of clergy and church people pulling in unity and harmony for the glory of God and for the peace of all classes in his liberated Diocese.

Into the history of the Church, and each church is but a community of Christians that go to make up the earthly cathedral of Jesus, flowed his whole life. From the pens of those who observed and appraised him come the key notes of this biography, and the greatest of these

testimonials as to his right to be crowned The Virginia
Bishop is the evidence in him of oneness with God:
"Bishop Johns gladly grasped the hand of every Christian
man as a brother in the faith. . . ." Mankind of his day
surely had "no such friend on earth," as John Johns.

The Rev. Dr. G. MacLaren Brydon, D.D., Historiographer of the Diocese of Virginia, writing in 1957, of
the *Highlights Along the Road of the Anglican Church,*
declared "Bishop Johns the Defender and Protector of
the Church." Dr. Brydon writes that Bishop Johns ". . .
because of the devotion of his people, was enabled upon
two different occasions to save the Episcopal Church
and the Diocese of Virginia from great calamity."

His successful effort brought the Diocese of war-
wrecked Virginia "back into the fellowship of the
Protestant Episcopal Church in the United States. . . .
He stood by himself at first (1865), but he won" in
May of 1866. Dr. Brydon goes on to relate, that:

"The second great contribution which Bishop Johns
made to the life of the Church was in the years 1873-75,
at the time when the (low church) radical element
(formed) the Reformed Episcopal Church, . . . There
was a general conviction that because of his influence
the majority of the clergy and people of the Diocese
would go with him . . . but John Johns stood firm as
a rock . . . (and in Virginia) the movement stopped
right there . . . the leaders of the Church in his generation knew that the stand taken by Bishop Johns had
saved the Church. . . ." John Johns, the emotionally
happy and physically vigorous pilot had brought his
war-torn ship into port.

Bishop Gibson, writing in about 1900, tells us that Bishop Johns was "a preacher of consummate power and polish . . . always spoke without notes . . . his voice was sweetened and extraordinarily flexible . . . blessed with an uncommon degree of health and vigor . . . his love of God and his fellow man seemed to increase. . . ." Think of the war-wrecked Parishes he helped rebuild, and of the cheer he personally carried on foot, on horseback, on boat, buggy and early railroad, to the "many darkened homes and broken hearts of his clergy and people." So convincing was the force of his Christian leadership that in his Diocese of Virginia "confirmations numbered a thousand or more every year," between the seventieth and eightieth years of his life.

Who was The Virginia Bishop—John Johns? After the Civil War he and General Robert E. Lee were among the best known and most loved men of Virginia. Dr. E. L. Goodwin, Historiographer of the Diocese of Virginia in 1923, wrote: "Bishop Johns was doubtless the greatest preacher, not even excepting Bishop Randolph, that the Church in Virginia has ever had."

Here's a man who was a man. Even when approaching seventy he raced forward on horseback from battlefield to battlefield, no more afraid of ambush or bullet than of the cross on a pulpit, for he practiced what he preached in the valley of the shadow of death. All his titles and honors before and after his name hardly tell the full story of a bishop on the loose in a battle area. Even the frontispiece is a living photograph of a loving, gentle man. No, this is not a book on Religion. It is a biography of THE VIRGINIA BISHOP.

CHAPTER
II

JOHN JOHNS IN MARYLAND

In 1819, All Saints' Parish was emerging from its age of confusion and John Johns, highly educated and mighty in physical and spiritual power, was poised at the beginning of his ministry eager to render at All Saints' Church his most devoted service to Christ and His Cross. Frederick Town, Maryland, a rural trading center in a fertile valley surrounded by gentle rolling hills, was a challenging place for young John Johns, for there he found waiting for him a rustic environment, a new love, a new set of friends, a new church and a very poor though happy way of life far removed from Delaware.

Frederick Town's twenty-five hundred people were "strong and positive characters," and also hospitable, industrious and devoted to their flourishing agricultural community of brick and stone row houses and stores. Strung out for a few blocks from the crossing of the East-West National Pike and the North-South Seneca Trail, it was a healthy and wide-awake town of many fine denominations, including German Reformed, German Lutheran, Roman Catholic, Baptist and Methodist. All Saints' Episcopal Church, built between 1814 and 1818 to replace its old Colonial Church, was eager to welcome a Rector so high in hope and rich in youth.

About 1815 the leaders at the Bar in Frederick Town were Francis Scott Key, his brother-in-law, Roger Brooke

Taney, a Roman Catholic who later became Chief Justice of the Supreme Court of the United States, Key's cousin, Arthur Shaaff, old Justice of the Supreme Court of the United States and first Governor of Maryland, General Thomas Johnson, and, for young Johns in 1819, the most important lawyer was Governor Johnson's prosperous brother, Colonel Baker Johnson. Baker Johnson, born in Calvert County, Maryland on September 30, 1747, had married Miss Catharine Worthington, the lovely daughter of Col. Nicholas Worthington of Anne Arundel County, Maryland. One of their children was Miss Julianna, who on November 20, 1820 became young John Johns' most precious partner in his new-found Parish.

There in a little frontier town of Maryland, stood the bridegroom, a physical, intellectual and spiritual giant! He was ready, capable and eager to run a race with the unconstitutional Compromise of 1820, past the complacent Compromise of 1850, into a college rent and closed by a challenge to a duel between faculty members, on foot and horseback right through the bloodiest battles of the Civil War and on to the long-delayed ending of Reconstruction in Virginia, in 1876 —the year this runner crossed the other threshold of his life into Heaven.

Frederick Town, on a night when the country "back inhabitants" came to do their dealing and feuding, could bestir itself into quite a bizarre place; but this newcomer from an exclusive college and an aristocratic family was no boyish parson with a timid soul. Rough Germans, high-tempered fighting Irishmen, bull-headed Scotsmen and even Roman Catholics in time began to shuffle into young Johns' church to listen to one of the greatest orators of all time. His hands were as large and powerful as those they clasped. His tongue and smile were mightier than any two fists.

Shortly after 1801 All Saints' Parish had been re-organized by William M. Beall, and "the Lawyer-Poet," Francis Scott Key, had become a member "of the struggling parish." Between 1768 and 1815 this plain brick House of Worship had no regular minister. Shortly after 1742, when Frederick Town was still a frontier Colonial Parish, All Saints' Church was located on a hill with mud and wet marshland all around it, a most uninviting location in the southern segment of the town. Col. Baker Johnson was a member of the Vestry of All Saints' from 1801 to 1811.

In June of 1791, when the old Braddock Road of 1755 was free of mud, George Washington left Georgetown at 4 a.m. and reached Frederick Town by sundown. I doubt if travelling had improved any between 1791 and the time (1819 to 1829) John Johns remained at All Saints' Church. Actually, between 1732—when the fifth Lord Baltimore granted the fertile soil of the present City of Frederick to wealthy Patrick Dulany— and 1829, travelling had improved only from an ancient Seneca Indian trail to a rough stagecoach road; and all of that forty miles from Frederick, through my home town of Gaithersburg, Maryland, to Washington, D. C., was not paved until after the beginning of our World War I.

All Saints' Church, from the Rev. Joseph Jennings in

1742 to this date, has, with two exceptions, had outstanding rectors. There were twenty in all. During, or
shortly before the 1746 to 1758 incumbency of Rev.
Samuel Hunter, the brick Colonial Church, with brick
floors, high-back pews and no heat except that supplied
by "wooden boxes lined with tin, with an iron draw
that held about a tin cup of coals," was built on a hill
on East All Saints' Street. The Rev. Thomas Bacon,
compiler of "Bacon's Laws of Maryland," served from
1758 to 1768. (His wife was "the divorced wife of a
bigamous husband.") This Rev. Thomas Bacon had been
the chaplain to Lord Baltimore, that choice convert to
the Episcopal Church.

In 1766 a handsome rascal named Rev. Bennett Allen
arrived at Annapolis from England. While at Annapolis,
enjoying good liquor and pretty women, he exhibited
his "ungovernable temper" by challenging Samuel Chew
to a duel and later by attempting to cane Walter Dulany.
All Saints' refused to "surrender to him the keys of the
church," so he operated from Hagerstown for some in-
definite time after 1768. Allen never ceased to slander
Daniel Dulany, and finally in England, Allen killed
Lloyd Dulany in a duel, for which conduct it is believed
that Mr. Allen ended life as "a street beggar in London."

The Maryland Bill of Rights of 1776 put an end to
the silly supremacy of the Anglican Catholic Church of
England, in Maryland. After 1776, Episcopalians had
to get along on their own voluntary contributions, and
no longer depend on the Sheriff collecting "a tax of
forty pounds of tobacco from each male inhabitant" to
support one privileged State-Church. In a sense our

American Revolution was a Second Protestant Reformation.

Between 1785 and 1813, Rev. Bower tried to come to All Saints' once a month from Hagerstown, but drink and opium finally bottled him up in Hagerstown. All Saints' Parish, from 1766 to the coming of Rev. Frederick W. Hatch in 1815, staggered through the dark ages of religious confusion in America. Between 1814 and 1818, it built a new church, the expense of which fell most heavily on its poor rector, Mr. Hatch, who, because of starvation wages, was forced to leave in 1819.

A few weeks after his ordination the young Rev. John Johns was on a visit to Garrison Forest, and preaching at old St. Thomas Church near Baltimore when his friend Dr. Henshaw, "afterward Bishop of Rhode Island," who no doubt had read the newspaper advertisement of All Saints' Church in the *Frederick Herald,* made an appointment for Johns to preach at that church. It so happened that a minister from Virginia and John Johns arrived at All Saints' Church on the same Sunday, and I am very much inclined to believe that the Virginian probably was rejected in favor of John Johns of Delaware. That Virginian was none other than the Rev. William Meade, afterward the third Bishop of Virginia. The Rev. Edward L. Goodwin, D.D., Historiographer of the Diocese of Virginia, wrote in 1923, that Dr. Gibson in 1885 had quoted "a notice from the Frederick Herald of August 7, 1819 that 'The Rev. John Johns and the Rev. William Meade are expected in town tomorrow, when the Protestant Episcopal Church will be opened for Divine service.' " *The Virginia Churchman,* Vol. 39, No. 4, April, 1923.

Frederick in 1819 was a poor frontier area of Maryland, and I wonder why neither John Johns, nor his brother Henry Van Dyke Johns, ever returned to a church in their native state of Delaware. Anyway, John Johns learned of the opening at All Saints' from a mere newspaper advertisement, and let us now turn to chapters nine and ten, of the *History of All Saints' Parish,* Frederick, Maryland, and read what its Registrar, Mr. Helfenstein, therein reported, in 1932, as to the inherited and environmental qualities of two young men in the ministry: The Rev. John Johns and his brother, The Rev. Henry V. D. Johns. Here again you will read the mere reference to Bishop Johns' "refined and cultivated family" but no disclosure of the name of his father who in 1819 was the aristocratic and wealthy Chief Justice of Delaware.

Ernest Helfenstein in his *History of All Saints' Parish,* Chapter IX, says: "Immediately after the acceptance of the resignation of Mr. Hatch the following advertisement was inserted in the Frederick newspaper:

'The church being vacant by the resignation of Mr. Hatch, the vestry have appointed the first day of September next for the election of a Rector of this church and invite the attention of the clergy until that period.

By order of the vestry.

D. Schley, Reg'r'

and, on the day named, the Rev. John Johns, a deacon

aged 23 years, was unanimously elected rector of the parish. He was a native of Delaware, a graduate of Princeton, and had been ordained deacon by Bishop White on May 6, 1819. Having been brought up in the bosom of a refined and cultivated family, Mr. Johns was placed in the most favorable circumstances for his development and by his natural gifts was 'fashioned to much honor.' He immediately and completely won the affections of his people . . . and from the beginning of his career he took high rank as a preacher. When he took charge of Frederick he always began to write his sermon on Monday morning, finished it by Wednesday evening and began to commit it to memory Thursday morning but this habit he later discontinued and instead wrote his sermons on his mind. As an illustration of his effectiveness as a preacher, the story is told that, at one of the services in All Saints' Mr. John Thompson Brooke, 'a Roman Catholic' and 'a bright and rising lawyer,' entered the church, more to scoff than to worship but was converted under the attractive preaching of Mr. Johns and, entering the ministry, he became an eminent and eloquent clergyman. A reference to Mr. Johns says: 'We may truly say that to John Johns, God gave five talents—a bright intellect, an emotional nature, natural earnestness, a melodious voice and facility and felicity of speech.' In addition to these personal qualities of heart and mind, the hold of Mr. Johns upon the love and interest of his people was strengthened by his marriage to Julianna, daughter of Col. Baker and Catharine Worthington Johnson; and, after his advancement to the priesthood in All Saints' Church, on July 26, 1820, by Bishop Kemp, this happy relationship between pastor and people continued to exist for almost ten years.

"Although the chief characteristic of Mr. Johns was that of a loving and lovable pastor, he was not wanting in administrative ability . . . largely through the influence of Mr. Johns, the financial condition was placed upon a firmer basis than it had been. The unsatisfactory system of remuneration of the rector was corrected by an agreement to pay Mr. Johns a stated salary of $900.00 . . .

"Probably the most important accomplishment of Mr. Johns was his organization of the parish Sunday School which convened at eight o'clock in the morning . . .

"Another item of interest in connection with Mr. Johns' administration was his proposition to form a parochial library . . . The response to this was both prompt and liberal . . .

"At all times during his administration, Mr. Johns received the loyal support of his vestry which was composed of

John Grahame	William Goldsborough
William Tyler	John Dill
William Ross	William B. Tyler
Richard Potts	John Nelson

and no rector could have received a greater degree of faithful cooperation and appreciation than was bestowed upon him by members of his congregation. This appreciation was shown in a material way by the increase in his salary from $900.00 to $1,200.00 and convincing evidence of the response to his labors appears in the personnel of the class presented by him for confirmation on October 4, 1827: Males—8; Females—16; 'Persons of Color'—5.

"After nine years of service in All Saints' Church, the ability of Mr. Johns had become so recognized, both within and out of the parish, that his services were sought for larger and more important fields. Calls '(not to Delaware but)' to Philadelphia and Baltimore had been received and declined, but a new call to Christ Church, Baltimore, came to him with such an appeal and offered such opportunities for service that he felt compelled to accept it and accordingly his resignation was presented to the vestry of All Saints' on July 21, 1828 and accepted with assurances 'that official separation will occasion no abatement of gratitude for your kind and acceptable services or of personal attachment for yourself and family.'

"After leaving Frederick, Mr. Johns continued his successful ministry in Baltimore where in 1837 a new church was built for him on Gay Street. Large as this church was, it was filled every Sunday and he was then considered the best preacher in the city. . . ."

Dr. Packard wrote that the Rev. Dr. John Thompson Brooke, father of the Rev. Pendleton Brooke and the Right Rev. Francis Key Brooke, Bishop of Oklahoma, "had the power to prepare and arrange even the very language of an elaborate sermon, and with rare eloquence and clearness deliver it unwritten, exactly as it had been prepared. Bishop Johns alone surpassed him in this rare gift."

It was the preaching of the Rev. John Johns that in-

spired the Rev. Dr. John Thompson Brooke, a young
Roman Catholic lawyer in the office of Roger Brooke
Taney of Frederick Town, Maryland, to abandon the law
and enter the newly opened Theological Seminary at
Alexandria, Virginia, in 1823. Dr. Brooke died about
1861.

Chief Justice Roger Brooke Taney, a Roman Catholic,
married the sister of Francis Scott Key, a loyal Episcopalian, and a pew in All Saints' Episcopal Church was
in Justice Taney's name although Justice Taney never
left the Roman Catholic Church. Incidentally, Roger
Brooke Taney and Anne Phoebe Charlton Key made
one promise to the Catholic Priest to get him to marry
them, and a secret ante-nuptial promise between themselves as to their children; namely, all sons to be
brought up as Roman Catholics and all daughters to
remain Episcopalians.

Mr. Ernest Helfenstein tells us that "this difference
in religion was, by agreement, never discussed by husband
and wife and never in any way marred the happiness
of an unusually happy life. So sure was each that the
other was a Christian that no doubt ever suggested itself
to either that they would not meet in Heaven . . . Four
of the children of this union were daughters, one a
son, and the agreement was faithfully respected." Chief
Justice Taney of Dred Scott fame was tall, and thin,
and ugly, while Anne was petite and lovely. Their marriage on January 7, 1806, at Pipe Creek Plantation, so
we are told by my learned friend Judge Edward S.
Delaplaine, was jovially referred to as "the union of
a hawk with a sky-lark." Delaplaine, *Francis Scott Key,*

ANN VAN DYKE JOHNS
Mother of Bishop Johns

20a

The Three Johns Brothers

REV. JOHN JOHNS
From Painting by Miss Peale

REV. HENRY V. D. JOHNS

KENSEY JOHNS, IV, LL.D.
Chancellor of Delaware

p. 47. In Chapter X, Helfenstein further says as to the Rev. Henry V. D. Johns:

"The desire of the congregation to show its appreciation of Mr. John Johns by increases in salary was its expression of devotion; but, . . . with the belief that a successor of equal ability would not be obtained, the vestry" reduced the salary to "$800.00, with an allowance of $150.00 for rent of a parsonage . . ."

The Rev. Henry V. D. Johns arrived in Frederick, September 14, 1832.

"Mr. Johns was a native of Delaware and brother of his predecessor, the Rev. John Johns. Having graduated from Princeton and the General Theological Seminary, he was ordained deacon by Bishop White in 1826. Although not of a robust constitution, Mr. Johns was an able preacher of the intellectual type, . . . he was a faithful pastor of an affectionate and endearing disposition, which soon won for him a place in the affections of his people second only to that previously enjoyed by his brother . . ." In 1836 ". . . he moved to St. Andrew's Church, in Baltimore, . . . Mr. Johns later succeeded his brother at Christ Church, in the same city."

". . . in the thirteen years which had elapsed since the departure of Mr. John Johns, . . . the congregation had been served by five different clergymen for varying lengths of time . . ."

"This continued use of a small plot for nearly one hundred years had exhausted its capacity . . . Thus passed the old parish burying ground . . . amongst those buried there were General Thomas Johnson, First Governor of Maryland, and his brother Joshua Johnson, first U. S.

Consul to London and the father of Mrs John Quincy
Adams; the wife of John Hanson, theoretically the first
President of the United States; . . . Mary Lavinia Johns,
infant daughter of Rev. Henry V. D. Johns and Lavinia
Johns; . . . John Henry Johns, infant son of Rev. John
and Julianna Johns; . . . Baker Johnson; . . . Thomas W.
Johnson, M.D. . . .," etc.

Bishop Johns' brother, the Rev. Henry V. D. Johns,
was the first rector of Trinity Church, built in 1829 on
Fifth Street, Washington, D. C. Born, October 23, 1803,
at Newcastle, Delaware, "between the hours of 11 and
12 o'clock in the morning," married, 1827, Lavinia, the
daughter of Colonel William and Fidelia (Rogerson)
Montgomery, the Rev. Dr. Henry Van Dyke Johns was
Rector of the old Christ Church and the first Rector of
Emmanuel Church, of Baltimore, Maryland. "Ten thousand people attended his funeral on foot, for he was
greatly beloved." He died on Good Friday, April 22,
1859.

On January 3, 1856, the Rt. Rev. Dr. John Johns,
D.D., LL.D., Assistant Bishop of Virginia and former
rector of the parish, was present to give inspiration and
a dynamic impetus to the opening of the third, and most
beautiful, All Saints' Church, in Frederick, Maryland.

The streets of Frederick have been trod by several
dedicated and famous missionaries of our Church. The
Rev. Joshua Peterkin, as lovely a man as ever served God,
was there from 1841 to 1845, and it was then that his
barefooted son, George, developed in that glory of honest
poverty which carried him through the Civil War and
on to become that most loved first "Mountain" Bishop

of West Virginia. If one admires military men who left the ministry to punish God's children, then one certainly can jump to attention and salute that brave and efficient graduate of West Point, Professor of Mathematics and Rector of All Saints' Church, the Rev. William Nelson Pendleton, who rushed out of the pulpit at Lexington, Virginia, to become a Major General and Chief of Artillery of the Army of Northern Virginia, under General Robert E. Lee. His men were so accurate that General Pendleton would shout: "Lord have mercy on their souls! Fire!" After the war he became rector of Lee's Episcopal Church, at Lexington, Virginia. His grandfather was Colonel Hugh Nelson, of Yorktown, Va.

The time has come for the pen to aim its point at the Christian leaders of America—men who placed their love and devotion to the Cross of Jesus above their own personal concept of patriotism. And Bishop Johns did serve God in Maryland and in Virginia, and in the South he was a servant of God, and not a soldier engaged in internecine conflict, for which Jesus must love him. Young men of each generation must see that their most manly choice and greatest opportunity for service above self are to be found in the ranks of marching Christian servants of the Lord.

The next word picture of the Rev. John Johns comes from the pen of Dr. E. L. Goodwin, as it appears in the April, 1923 issue of *The Virginia Churchman:*

"Mr. Johns, by his marked ability and exalted character, quickly won recognition throughout the Church in Maryland, and his pronounced evangelical views made him a leader of the 'Low Church' party of that

Diocese . . . In 1828 Bishop Kemp died, and the Convention which met that year was called upon to elect his successor. The candidate selected by the High Church party was the Rev. Dr. William E. Wyatt, rector of St. Paul's Church, Baltimore, . . . The Low Churchmen united upon Mr. Johns, then but thirty-two years of age and rector of a small town parish . . . Three ballots were taken by the clergy, on each of which Mr. Johns received a majority but failed of the necessary two-thirds. The election was then deferred for a year. During this year Mr. Johns accepted a call to Christ Church, Baltimore. This was the first Christ Church, situated far down town on Baltimore Street. In 1829 the Convention met again to try to elect a Bishop. Five ballots were taken without success and they again adjourned. The next year a compromise was effected by the appointment of a nominating committee who proposed the name of Dr. W. M. Stone, classed as a moderate High Churchman, who was elected; and the land had rest, comparatively speaking, for seven years.

"Johns meanwhile occupied himself vigorously with his pastoral duties. He soon became widely and most favorably known, and gained the reputation of being the best preacher in the city. His church was filled to overflowing, especially at night, and in 1837 his congregation built a new and very large church further up town on Gay Street, which was also soon filled. When the present Christ Church was built much further up town this church was bought for a down town mission church and continued for many years under the rectorship of Dr. Penick, until his election as Missionary

Bishop to Africa, and then of Dr. Peregrine Wroth. It was burned, if we mistake not, during the great Baltimore fire, and a new church was erected on its site which in turn has lately been sold, being now in the heart of the business district.

"Dr. Johns' fame as an evangelical preacher went abroad and he was in frequent demand for services outside of his own congregation and city. Early in 1838 Bishop Stone passed away, and in May the Convention met to elect a bishop with party lines drawn as strictly as ever before. . . . Again Dr. Wyatt and Dr. Johns were placed in nomination for the episcopate by their respective friends. But they had anticipated such an event and Dr. Wyatt, as the spokesman of both, explained that they had determined together that they would not be the involuntary instruments of a disunion which they both deplored. They then united in placing in nomination Dr. Alonzo Potter, afterwards Bishop of Pennsylvania. This proposition did not please the friends of Dr. Johns, and the clergy proceeded to ballot with these gentlemen again unwillingly pitted against each other. Nine ballots were taken, the Low Churchman having usually a majority but without being able to secure the necessary two-thirds vote. Finally the expedient of nomination by a committee was again resorted to. The committee appointed brought in the names of two clergymen of New York and one of these, Dr. Eastburn, afterwards Bishop of Massachusetts, was finally chosen. He declined the election, and a special Convention was called. Once more Drs. Wyatt and Johns were placed in nomination and eleven ballots were taken with the usual indecisive result. At last both of these gentlemen addressed the Convention and positively declined being considered as candidates. Dr. Wyatt then nominated Missionary Bishop Kemper and Dr. Johns seconded his name, and he was elected, but afterwards declined to accept. Nearly two years later Bishop Whittingham was elected and consecrated."

CHAPTER
III

BISHOP JOHNS IN VIRGINIA

From 1823 to 1827 the young Theological Seminary in Virginia stood on the main street of the dirty river-port city of Alexandria close by the market place where God's servants are most needed, where the politicians go for votes, and where evangelical ministers must go to convert souls. But the speech-deadening noise of the stagecoach's iron-tired wheels, the yelling of street vendors, and the pounding of iron shod horses' hoofs on the cobblestone streets as they passed by at a trot, forced the Seminary to retreat to a more quiet location on "The Hill," outside of Alexandria. However, during that infant period, down on the sidewalks of Alexandria, were trained many stout hearts and brilliant minds of the Episcopal clergy of that day.

One of those early soldiers of the Church was Bishop Johns' cousin, the Rev. Leonard H. Johns (1805-1868), as to whom the History of the Seminary contains this brief reference: "Johns, Leonard H.; 1826. Maryland; Par. priest and college professor, d. 186— . . ." Professor at Newton University, Baltimore, he married Henrietta Geiger. His father, Leonard Hollyday Johns, born in 1779, married Margaret Williams, February 10, 1801, in nearby Montgomery County, Maryland. The grounds on which the White House now stands were part of the estate of Col. Thomas Johns, grandfather of the Rev. Leonard Hollyday Johns.

27

During all those early years, two of the most faithful members of the Education Society's Board of Directors were Francis Scott Key, Esquire, and the Rev. John Johns, the latter elected in 1824. It was as early as 1825, on motion of the Rev. John Johns of Fredericktown, Maryland, that the Seminary required that each candidate for admission present a college diploma, or pass special examinations on philosophy, rhetoric, Latin, Greek, etc. Every young minister must be emotionally healthy, physically vigorous, and highly educated.

In 1825, the Rev. John Johns, of "Frederick County, Md.," Francis Scott Key, Esq., the "lawyer poet" and tithing Christian, then of Georgetown, D. C., and others, were elected "Managers." Often the Society met at the Church of the Presidents, as St. John's Church, Washington, D. C., is popularly called. In 1826, the Rev. John Johns, of Frederick, Md., was serving as Fourth Vice President; also in 1827, and again in 1831, when another one of the elected Managers was the Rev. John Johns' brother, the Rev. Henry Van Dyke Johns, of Washington, D. C. By 1842, the Rev. Dr. John Johns, D.D., had been elected First Vice President, and this is the year he was consecrated Assistant Bishop of Virginia.

At the Semi-Centennial anniversary of the Seminary in 1873, Bishop Johns, then seventy-six years of age, proudly looked out upon the procession as it was formed under the direction of the Rev. Arthur Shaaff Johns (1843-1921), of the Class of 1873, only child by his marriage in 1838 to Margaretta Jane Shaaff, daughter of Dr. John Thomas (1763-1819) and Mary (Sydebotham, 1776-1810) Shaaff, of Georgetown, D. C. Dr. and Mrs.

Shaaff also were the parents of Arthur Shaaff II, who married Mary A. Forsyth, and had Captain Francis Key Shaaff. Elsewhere in this inspiring history of the Theological Seminary, we read: "Johns, Arthur S., D.D.; 1873, Virginia; Washington; Sec'y of the Diocese. Deputy to four Gen. Convs. d. 1921, aet. 80. Son of Bp. Johns." Son Arthur Shaaff Johns was born October 10, 1843.

In these ramblings, I have hinted that Virginians were prejudiced in favor of having other Virginians serve as their bishops, yet even in 1824, there was springing up in Virginia a feeling of respect for Episcopalians of Maryland, especially for our physically vigorous and well-educated John Johns. Although the history of the Seminary, from which I am quoting at random, most conspicuously does not stress the fact, nevertheless, John Johns was born in New Castle, Delaware, so Virginia became his adopted state and there he remade his own environment. He was not a Southerner. He had no Southern background. At the time of the Civil War, he was the only Southern Bishop who had not been born in Virginia or in the Carolinas; therefore, he was a Yankee Bishop.

Some day I hope people will see me in my daughter, and know me by her Christian deportment, because the closest I can come to knowing the heart and soul Bishop John Johns is through the influence his devoted daughter exerted on her little Sunday School children. The Rt. Rev. James A. Winchester, D.D., of the Class of 1877, tells us that

"Down the vista of years, I see a picture, embody-

ing an inspiration that still moves my soul. Miss
Julia Johns, daughter of 'the beloved John Johns'
(Bishop of Virginia), was one of the teachers in
the Sunday School that gathered in the Seminary
building. She had nine boys in her class. During the
summer her nephew, Henry Peyton died . . .

"Is it strange when I visit the Seminary Hill that I
should go to the sacred little Cemetery and fall on
my knees at Miss Julia Johns' grave and thank God
for her abiding influence upon my life? In these
days of agitation about 'Church Schools' I see nothing equal to the work that holy woman accomplished
upon the nine boys, drawing them by chords of
love to that Blessed Saviour Whom we knew she
consistently served. I get a glimpse of the vanished
doubts, driven away by her loving counsel, and there
comes a thrill that inspired my college course in
subsequent years. It was my spiritual privilege to be
a member of her household after I had the high
honor of acting as pall bearer at her father's funeral.
My dear room-mate there in her home was C.
Braxton Bryan, an encyclopaedia of knowledge and a
spiritual giant. We felt that the shadows of the great
Bishop, who had laid his hands on my head in confirmation, rested upon us . . ."

In 1958, Dean Trotter, of the Episcopal Theological
Seminary in Virginia, generously presented me with a
set of the History of that Seminary, and later he wrote
to me that the work of Miss Julianna Johns "resulted in
the eventual founding of the Alexandria Hospital."

Through the pages of the *History of the Episcopal Seminary in Virginia,* I have searched in vain for some human interest story about Bishop Johns, his parents, his three wives and his seven children. Hardly any mention is made in the running accounts of this work of the fact that he was born in New Castle, Delaware. A few touching words about his daughter, Miss Julianna, born January 3, 1822, who, of all his family, lies buried with her father, and two brief mentions of his son, the Rev. Dr. Arthur S. Johns. "His coming to Seminary Hill in 1854 from Williamsburg, Virginia," proved a great blessing to the Institution. "His family added a rich contribution to the social life of 'The Hill.' Bishop Johns, who had been living at 'Malvern' on 'The Hill,' moved 'during the Civil War' (in May of 1861) to the neighborhood of Richmond."

Richmond, Virginia, a busy inland city of hills, watermelons, diversified industry and many monuments, endures intensely hot tobacco weather in the summer and chilling-to-the bone rains, with occasional snow, in the winter. White folks and black folks love their Capital City located a two hours' easy ride from Norfolk, and, prior to about 1900, separated from Washington, D. C., by difficult-to-cross swamps and rivers. Richmond was a natural place for the Capital of the Confederacy after Virginia had seceded from the Union. Jamestown had been the first seat of the Established Church and of the Royal Colony. Nathaniel Bacon, about 1675, rebelled against the neglect of Royal Governor Berkeley to spend enough of the tobacco profits on protection of the frontiersmen from the Indians, and between 1699 and 1779, Williamsburg, the second Colonial Capital, became the gathering place for the great planter aristocracy until the Revolution, when patriots and frontiersmen wrested the Capital from its royal mooring and located it at Richmond.

By the time of the War Between the States, it had become the socially correct thing for most proper white folks to be Episcopalians, even though for years it was the Baptists, Presbyterians and Methodists who held the whip hand over both Unitarian and Episcopalian. When it came time for Jefferson Davis to be inaugurated President of the Confederacy, Bishop Meade was too ill to do the honors, so Bishop Johns was fetched to lend his presence to the pomp and ritual of that tragic pageant of history. The sun did not shine upon that solemn event, for it rained so hard and turned so cold, that both Bishop Johns and President Jefferson Davis were soaked and chilled by the worst of February's rains; even so, that ominous stroke of nature in no way restrained the high spirits and stout hearts of the assembled audience. Bishop Johns administered the oath of office to Jefferson Davis and the last touch of secession was completed on the Holy Bible held by the hand of a Virginia Bishop of the Episcopal Church, who was not a Southerner.

Davis' family had been hard-shell Baptist, who, like those followers of Robert Brown and of the Separatist Mayflower Pilgrims, had staggered under the heel of the Church of England. In 1608, an angry Anglican Catholic mob had stoned the Separatist Pilgrims as they sought to flee from England to gain religious freedom in Holland. Possibly the society-loving Mrs. Davis, the new First Lady of the South, a true and correct Episcopalian, had not been too overjoyed by the Harper's Ferry antics of John Brown of Ossawatomie, said to have been the riotous descendant of Peter Browne, the thirty-third signer of the Mayflower Compact, America's first democratic constitution. (I doubt if Peter Browne had any sons.) Actually, it was Colonel Robert E. Lee who put an end to the 1859 riot of fanatical John Brown, who promptly got his neck stretched for all his dedicated trouble in attempting to free the slaves.

Professor Channing once jokingly told me that it was the Southern ladies who almost won the Civil War, because so many of the Union soldiers fell in love with those beautiful girls and deserted the Federal forces. Southern women had a way of ruling a man's heart, purse, and religion. Anyway, it was the socially correct thing for the ruling classes of Virginia to be Episcopalians, and no sooner had Mrs. Davis reached Richmond than she saw to it that Baptist Jeff became baptized at the Executive Mansion, and confirmed in the Episcopal Church by Bishop John Johns. Even as the President was being confirmed at St. Paul's Church* (prior to the war, the socially elite had moved from St. John's Church of Patrick Henry fame; to Monumental Church; to St Paul's Church), the enemy's gunboats were poking their noses into the James River to draw down the curtain of peace and begin the siege of war on Richmond.

THE WAR YEARS

When the Civil War came, John Johns was the consecrated Assistant Bishop of a Diocese that happened to

---

* Cornerstone laid by Bishop Johns.

have been Virginia, and his first loyalty was pledged to God. Of course his choice was simple. He said: "I have never for a moment had the slightest misgiving as to my choice," and after all, had not loyalty to the Union been rather fluid between 1787 and 1861? As you follow his war errands of mercy from battlefield to battlefield, remember that he was a man of sixty-five in 1861 and in his seventieth year in 1865, fearlessly riding horseback, and often alone, to the various battlefields where his people needed him the most.

On April 12, 1861, trigger-happy South Carolinians drew straws for the "kick" of being the first to fire at defenseless Fort Sumter, more to incite Virginia into seceding than to start a war; and do not forget that between 1804 and 1823 the North had been almost as violently determined to secede. On April 30, 1861, Mayor Fernando Wood and his City Council were all for the secession of Manhattan Island and Long Island with New York City being declared a "free city," so it could control the commerce of a divided New World. Selfish Baltimore merchants craved cotton commerce more than they loved the Union. There was no moral reason why Bishop Johns, a clergyman, needed to take sides. As he said: "Christians are to be peacemakers," and he merely practiced what he preached.

Ah, but on second thought the northern industrialists— those cravers after war profits and a high tariff—whipped up mob hysteria over the South having fired, not at the Union, but on the flag; and their wealth-loving counterpart, the great planters (there may have been 350,000 slaveholders in the South), to save their feudal plantation system and their investment in slavery, let loose a counter-hysteria: Southerners, rise up, not in defense of "King Cotton" and three and a half million slaves but in self-defence! Once started, it was a Civil War of seven million Southerners against twenty-one million not-too-enthusiastic Northerners. Lofty patriotic concepts never were at a lower ebb—Lincoln and his party had no desire to free a nation of the sin of slavery, or concern itself with slave labor that held three-fourths of the Southern people in poverty. Bishop Johns' call of duty was never clearer. He remained to minister to the souls of mankind in Virginia. Lincoln's chief objective was to save the Union. Johns' chief objective was to serve God.

Enlightened opinion in America knew, as Francis Preston Blair wrote in 1856, that "the South could not marshal a force equal to one-third that of the North; . . . (they) cannot command one-third the men or money or marine force the North can wield," with a population ratio of about seven to twenty-one million. Bishop Johns no doubt realized that the South was being propagandized into war by a mere four hundred thousand slaveholders of about four million slaves. But three-fourths of the Southern people were slow in realizing that slave labor kept the non-slave-holding white population in poverty, and this competition was especially depressing on the poor white folks of the cotton states. Once the war broke, most Virginians found themselves fighting in pure self-defence with almost no help coming from Maryland, Western Virginia, Kentucky or Missouri. Lincoln sealed off those border states prior to the First Battle of Bull Run, as a part of the Anaconda Plan, of Virginia's own "Old

Fuss and Feathers," Union General Winfield Scott (1786-1866).

The Civil War for the South was a twofold blessing. It abolished a legalized form of wealth—the human slave, and it also abolished economic slavery, both vicious evils of the plantation system. The blood of youth, both South and North, cleansed a foul Union.

The War to Cleanse the Union brought forth a professor of physics and drill tactics at V. M. I. who also found time to conduct a Sunday School for negroes in Lexington, Virginia, and molded him into an everlasting symbol of Christian character. He was one who was more afraid of alcohol than of bullets, one who rose at 6:00 a.m. and knelt in prayer—he was "always praying," one whose guiding maxim was "Duty is ours; consequences are God's." Years later, a Catholic priest praying at the unveiling of this Presbyterian's monument was inspired to say: "And thou knowest, O Lord, that when thou didst decide that the Confederacy should not succeed thou hadst first to remove thy servant, Stonewall Jackson."

Bishop Johns and Stonewall Jackson had a deep respect for one another's fearless bravery. They converted souls on the battlefield, and some of those brave men Stonewall Jackson led on to Heaven.

"Gen. Jackson, just before his death, sent him (Bishop Johns) a special request to send, if possible, forty faithful ministers to supply that number of vacant chaplaincies in the army on the Rappahannock. Gen. Lee added his earnest request, and the Bishop appealed to the Council. By a solemn resolution the Bishop was asked to call

AMSTEL HOUSE, NEW CASTLE, DEL.

Here, on April 30, 1784, Kensey Johns married Ann Van Dyke, the fifteen year old daughter of Governor Nicholas Van Dyke.

36a

Transportation Prior to 1859

The De Witt Clinton Train which ran in 1830 between Albany and Schenectady

George Washington Locomotive, 1835

A typical scene in the Appalachian Mountains

Model of the John Stevens Locomotive. The first in America, 1825

Blockade of Engines at Martinsburg, Virginia

Coxey and his Army approaching Washington

AUTHOR'S NOTE—About 1914 I saw "General" Coxey, in an open carriage, with a dozen followers on horseback, as he made his second trip to Washington, D. C. I never shall forget his gentle manners and his gracious smile, as he sat there talking to me.

36b

OLD COURT HOUSE, NEWCASTLE, DEL.

Some Christian Leaders

ROGER WILLIAMS.

COTTON MATHER.

SAMUEL KIRKLAND.

WM. G. BROWNLOW.

JOHN CARROLL.

LEONIDAS POLK.

HARRIET BEECHER STOWE.

WILLIAM E. CHANNING.

JOHN TAYLOR.

36d

upon the ministers then without Parishes to render religious services to the army for such a time and at such a place as he might designate; and the whole clergy of the Council, in a body, offered themselves for the work," so wrote Bishop Gibson.

April of 1861 found Bishop Johns riding his long circuit along the Ohio River, and here is what he wrote:

"At Wheeling the painful intelligence which reaches us from the East strongly inclined me to return. This feeling was increased at Parkersburg, but as I could obtain no reply to a telegram I sent to Alexandria, I resolved to keep on until I was overtaken by some positive and decided information. This was not long in coming. It was brought down the river in the boat by which I left Ravenswood, but too late to change my direction. I therefore kept on to Point Pleasant, sixty miles—officiated there as above—took passage up the river at 2 a.m. on Thursday, April 25, and by traveling night and day reached the Seminary Hill by 10 p.m. the next day; though the usual route through Washington being obstructed, I was obliged to diverge at the Point of Rocks and return by way of Leesburg."

Almost any day in May, Alexandria, Virginia, can be like paradise. The air fresh, clean and cool; and on May 10, 1861, "the grass, lilacs, crocuses and lily of the valley never were more beautiful." The innocent rosebud, the blossoms on the fruit trees and the birds that sang that spring all told of how all nature was aglow in happiness but, alas, the people were bewildered and tense in their minds as they looked out over the Potomac to yonder Capitol dome, and heard the beginning of "Blow Bugle Blow—."

Mrs. Judith W. McGuire in her peace-loving home now empty of men and young ladies, had begun her *Diary of a Southern Refugee.* On that 10th day of May she came upon Bishop Johns' wife, Angelina E. Southgate Johns, "packing up valuables" not willing to believe that all had to be left in tears to fate. On May 16 these ladies "sat at the Malvern windows spying the enemy as they sailed up and down the river" (Potomac). Bishop Johns was at a Church Convention in Richmond.

Bishop Johns wrote, "In two hours after the invasion I was on the road with those of my family who had not previously removed. We went forth, not knowing whither, but satisfied that we should find shelter and service where God had appointed. The first night we passed with our friends at Chantilly, who have since found it necessary to leave their beautiful residence at the mercy of hostile intruders."

Chantilly, now Dulles International Airport, was the first stopping place out of Alexandria. Mrs. General Lee was there, as were the McGuires, Bishop and Mrs. Johns and many others of the carriage brigade of fleeing women and older men. Fighting had broken out around Fairfax. Harpers Ferry was swarming with Confederates. The McGuires moved on to the then safer Valley, by way of Upperville and Paris. "The elite of the land is in the ranks," wrote Mrs. Judith McGuire, whose *Diary* gives to us a quite sparkling play-by-play of what the refugees experienced during the "new Rebellion." The American Revolutionary War, she always alluded to as the "old

Rebellion." A Richmond paper in 1868 declared of her story that "in truth, it is the best history of the war in Virginia." She captured the spirit of her time as that spirit moved by before her own eyes. At "Mountain View" near Millwood, Virginia, Bishop Meade thought only of the war. He declared that the righteousness of this Revolution exceeded that of 1775.

Bishop Johns' own account tells of his journey by carriage out of Chantilly: "Saturday brought us to Warrenton, already crowded with refugees. Here the Rev. Mr. and Mrs. Barten, though every room in the parsonage was occupied, insisted on accommodating us." The next day he preached in Warrenton, and on Monday "We proceeded to Rappahannock County, to the residence of Captain J. S. Green, then absent in the service of his country. Here we were most kindly received by Mrs. Green, and found a hospitable home during our sojourn in that county."

The mention of Captain J. S. Green suggests that the following may be of interest.

At some time prior to 1939 my Aunt Henrietta Byrne Garrett, named after her grandmother, Henrietta Johns South Byrne, had urged me to go call on our cousin Arthur Shaaff Johns' widow, who then lived at 3215 Adams Mill Road, N.W., Washington, D. C., which I declined to do. (As early as 1932 this Lot 46, Sq. 2605 was owned by Rosalie Van Dyke Johns.) However, in 1940 I wrote to one of my cousins who had known the Johns family and knew of my relationship to Bishop Johns, for some information as to where he and his sister (my great-grandmother) Henrietta Johns South

Byrne were born. She, Mrs. Fannie Amiss Platt, then of Florida, replied in part as follows: "My family's association with that family came about in this wise. One Col. John Shakelford Green (first cousin to General Ashby) bought a part of my Grandfather Amiss' estate in the then Culpeper County, Virginia. On it, he built a house (Forest Hill) and to that house he brought his bride, who was Miss Sarah Taylor, of Norfolk, Virginia. Every summer her family came up to visit and the young folks of the two places were constantly together. One of the visiting families was that of Bishop Johns." (He frequently preached at the little stone chapel, now the Baptist Church, of Amissville, Virginia.)

"Bishop Johns had a son, Arthur S. Johns (born 1843), who spent considerable time in that region and married there, Miss Helen Lane, from Gaines X Roads (now called Ben Venue), Rapp'k County, Virginia, between Amissville and Front Royal, Virginia. They had three children, Rosalie, a son named Shaaff, who was killed in a streetcar accident, and a son named John Lane Johns . . ."

On September 12, 1861, Bishop and Mrs. Johns reached "The Briars," where he conducted the marriage ceremony of the McGuires' daughter to a soldier there on furlough for two days. Mrs. McGuire had a reason for omitting most names, or for referring to them only by initial. The Federals delighted in stealing diaries and printing them in New York papers, but her account of the First Battle of Bull Run (first Manassas) was a classic no Northern paper would have dared print.

The North was painfully handicapped in obtaining

a leader because the best generals in the regular army went to the rescue of Virginia. In May, 1861, the Confederate Capital was moved from Montgomery, Alabama, to Richmond—the arsenal of the South—just 115 miles from Washington, D.C. Congress took to the "Forward to Richmond" slogan and Scott, a son of Richmond, Virginia, ordered General McDowell and his none-too-well-trained Union boys to wipe out General Beauregard's army at Manassas Junction. Lincoln had not taken into account the speed with which Stonewall Jackson did get to Manassas Junction, nor did Lincoln then realize that his hoped-for short war was a pipe dream: it took five Federals to match one Confederate fighting to save his own Mother, wife, children and home in Virginia. On-to-Richmond was to have been a picnic, not a panic. The Federals loved their wine, women and song, so wine, women and song followed McDowell's army out of Washington. The girls, many of whom were "pick-ups" in Washington, came in carriages loaded with their finest silk dresses for the great ball to be held in Richmond— "On-to-Richmond!" gaily yelled the girls.

Of course many of those silly girls were refined ladies. The amusing part of this episode is that the soldiers went first—yes, in both directions. I have heard several old ladies tell of their happy ride out toward Manassas, and of their riotous dash back to Washington, D. C. All those soldier-crazy females needed to have done was to calmly wait for their running beaus to clear the roads, and the Confederate gentlemen would have escorted the girls back to the Potomac. McDowell took one look at Stonewall Jackson and ordered a retreat, for which

McDowell was dismissed and "Old Fuss and Feathers" General Scott, got what was coming to him for having ordered green soldiers to venture upon the soil of his own native Virginia.

The First Battle of Bull Run was a hilarious panic. The Federals, with their ladies not far to the rear, took one gasping look at the business end of the South's guns— no bayonets were needed—and they turned and ran "flying back to Washington, in confusion and terror, pell-mell, in the wildest excitement . . . each bush to their disordered imagination contained a savage Confederate." Those bushes probably concealed females who had fainted and could run no further.

Why, it simply was disgraceful. Those women first threw their silken finery out of the carriages, then the gals jumped out to outrun the horses. The land never before, or since, has witnessed such a strip-tease performance: gals stripped down almost to the hide in order to run after their gallant Federal escorts, back to Washington.

The Federals ran so fast that they kicked rabbits and foxes out of their path, to show horrified rabbits, foxes and ladies how to run back to Washington, D. C. The sight of fleeing Federals abandoning their women-dates must have converted the whole Confederate Army to laughter but when ladylike little things began to fly in all directions, the Confederate gentlemen must have closed their eyes and fallen to the ground in roaring laughter. I can hear now some of those near naked runners first pretend modest disgust and then break down and laugh at their own war-time conduct, back in the days of their silly youth.

If you take a dim view of my overly colored story, then read Mrs. McGuire's more refined and immortal classic on the Federal retreat not after, but before, the First Battle of Bull Run. But there was no fun in the slaughter that came after the first battle of Manassas.

Dr. E. L. Goodwin tells us that during the summer of 1861 Bishop Johns "served the small congregations at Washington, Woodville and Amissville, in Rappahannock and officiated in the adjoining counties as he was able. The evening before the battle of Bull Run he preached to the soldiers in camp at Manassas, 'the last public service in which some of them were privileged to unite.' On the day of first Manassas he preached in St. James, Warrenton, 'within hearing of the cannon and within sight of the smoke of that eventful conflict.' At night he preached to the colored people, but the exercises were often interrupted by the intense excitement produced by tidings coming from the battle-ground. Two days later he delivered an address at the funeral of four soldiers, 'one of them the worthy officer on whose arm I had leaned just one week before while passing through encampment to the religious services which I have mentioned.' A little later he 'preached morning and afternoon at the headquarters of General Jackson, near Centerville.' He also preached in the hospitals whenever opportunity offered. In December of that year he moved to Richmond, and during the winter he preached regularly, when in the city, in St. Philip's Church, which had just been built for the colored people;

and was 'engaged daily, with increasing interest, in visiting the sick soldiers in our hospitals, ministering from cot to cot and assembling the convalescents for social worship.' "

In February, March and April, Bishop Johns was working in the hospitals of Richmond. On May 5, 1862 he preached at St. Paul's.

"In the spring of 1862 he moved with his family to Halifax county where he made his headquarters for the summer. But very soon 'the battles in front of Richmond which had now begun left (him) in no doubt as to the place of duty,' and he returned to his ministrations to 'the wounded and the dying.' The next fall he moved to Ashland, where two of his sons had found a temporary home. He found that young village crowded with refugees, and a public room large enough for services was put at his disposal for three Sundays in the month. Here he and the Rev. Dr. John P. McGuire established the first regular services of our Church, organized a Sunday school, and found that 'the indications are encouraging that in better days an interesting congregation may be organized.' He lived in Ashland for six months or more, and after that alternated between Richmond and Halifax. Personally, however, he was little at home. His visitations to such portions of the Diocese as could be reached often involved long and circuitous journeys but were never intermitted, and his spare time was largely given to the army."

Mrs. Judith W. McGuire fills in with this: "Sept. 4, 1862—Our victory at Manassas complete; the fight lasted three days. General Kearney was killed in a cavalry fight at Chantilly. Beautiful Chantilly has become a glorious battle-field."

Bishop Johns was a welcome guest at every camp, especially since most Confederate Generals were not ashamed of "being Christians, who loved God." General J. E. B. Stuart never swore or drank; a living example of courage and dignity, and many of his youthful raiders followed his example. The same can be said of Stonewall Jackson and of most of the Confederate Generals.

October 19, 1862, found a dozen or so refugees crowded into one little cottage in Ashland, where it cost less to live than in Richmond: Bishop Johns and his family; Major Kensey Johns and his wife; Lieutenant John Johns and his wife, who was the daughter, Mary Eleanore Mercer McGuire (1831-1918), of the Rev. John P. McGuire and his wife, Mrs. Judith W. McGuire. The Rev. John P. McGuire and Bishop Johns went into Richmond daily to the hospitals, as did the Johns sons.

On November 7, 1862, Bishop Johns attended a Church council at Augusta, Georgia. Each spring the North shouted: "On-to-Richmond," and Ashland, full of refugees, lay in their path from Fredericksburg.

In Ashland, new refugees from Fredericksburg slept, row on row, in each little cottage. Coffee $4.10 per pound and tea $20.00. Others lived in Richmond's damp and cold basements and even in boxcars. Many selfish, panic-stricken residents of Richmond closed their doors on the southern refugees. The roar of cannon and the cold of early winter came nearer and nearer; train loads of wounded arrived at Ashland, and then went on to Richmond. Only rain and mud could stop the Federals.

"The Bishop was with us all day" working on the wounded, filling and carrying pitchers, bowls, baskets, bandages; helping to cut dirt-caked clothes off open wounds; giving emergency relief to save dying boys, anything to comfort and to keep them alive until they reached that city of hospitals, profiteers and refugees, Richmond. The last face seen by many a boy-soldier was that of Bishop Johns.

Mrs. McGuire pens the spirit of Richmond: "Shouts of victory and wails for the dead and dying were strangely blended." Wounds so deep, and minie balls that could not be located, or removed. Many, many hospitals.

In January, 1863, Mrs. McGuire wrote: "Colonel Bradley Johnson (Confederate General Bradley Johnson) has been with us for some days. He is nephew to Bishop Johns. February 22—A very deep snow kept the Bishop and the Rev. John P. McGuire from making their daily trip to the hospitals and prisons in Richmond." Winter dragged on: March 15, 1863—"The Bishop preached on 'Repentance.'"

On April 2, 1863, the Bishop witnessed a riot staged by some women in Richmond. Inflated prices, soaring rentals, usurious interest and food speculators were too much for the poor to endure, although none actually starved. On Good Friday "The Bishop preached for us today most delightfully from the text: 'Jesus Christ and Him crucified'." On April 4, 1863: "The Bishop set off this morning for his spring visitations, which are becoming, alas! very circumscribed—so much of the diocese is in the hands of the enemy."

In July, Mrs. General Lee stopped over at the Johns-

McGuire cottage in Ashland, on her way to Hot Springs, "in a boxcar, fitted up to suit an invalid." Bishop and Mrs. Johns "returned home (to the Ashland cottage) August 10, 1863, from their long trip in the South-west . . . they barely escaped a raid at Wytheville." This little company of Ashland refugees moved into Richmond but profiteering drove room rent and food so high that the Bishop was forced to return to Halifax where he could live on his meager income, for the summer.

Dr. Goodwin continues: "Immediately after the Council of 1863 the Bishop visited the Army of the Rappahannock to make the arrangements contemplated by the action of the Council. He found the army on the move, and that it was impossible to make any arrangements in advance. The best that could be done was to follow it up and preach whenever there was a halt made. The next few days, however, were busy ones." In Bishop Johns' words:

"June 3. On my arrival at Hamilton's Crossing I was met by the Rev. J. McGill, chaplain of the 52d Virginia Regiment, who informed me that in the Rockbridge Artillery company, then encamped in the vicinity, but under orders to march in a few hours, there were several persons anxious to receive confirmation. The necessary arrangements were soon made, and at 5 p.m. in front of the residence of Mr. Marye, I preached to the members of that brave band, baptized one, and confirmed six of their number. Before the next dawn their tents had disappeared and they were moving to share in the terrible conflicts of the campaign.

"During the interval between my arrival and this

service I passed some time at Headquarters in communication with the honored and beloved Commander of the
Army of Northern Virginia, in reference to its religious
improvement to which his example and counsel happily
contributed . . .

"June 4. In company with Gen. Pendleton I rode out
to the Headquarters of Gen. Ewell, recently appointed
to the command vacated by the death of the lamented
Gen. Jackson. The interview assured me the more that
the good Providence and grace of God had prepared the
way most invitingly for the extension of the gospel in
the army. At 5 p.m. I preached to the 52d Va. Regiment
under an arbor, which, though very extensive, did not
cover the congregation. While we were engaged in the
services a courier arrived with orders to march at midnight.

"June 5. I preached near Grace Church, Caroline
County, to the division under command of Gen Heth.
With the men seated on the grass, and many of them
on the limbs of surrounding trees, I ministered to as
attentive and serious a congregation as I ever addressed.
I had announced another appointment to preach for them
the following day, but again while I was preaching a
courier came with the intelligence that the enemy had
opened up on our troops at Fredericksburg and were
crossing in force below the town. Gen Heth's command
was ordered up. They marched during the night, and
the next day when the hour of my appointment arrived,
there was not even a straggler to be found in the vicinity.
It was an anxious day . . . The next morning, accompanied
by the Rev. Mr. Friend, I rode to Hamilton's Crossing to

see if there would be an opportunity for public service, and if not, to be on hand to minister to the wounded, should a battle ensue. We found the troops in battle array, not knowing at what moment the enemy might attempt to advance. Very soon we were called upon by Col. Leaventhorpe, who commanded a North Carolina Regiment, who came to say that though his officers and men had been on the march during the night they would be thankful if we would conduct service for them. . . . Mr. Friend read the morning service and I addressed the congregation. Our appropriate psalms and hymns were accompanied by the music of a part of the regimental band which had been accustomed to render such assistance with the Rev. Aristides Smith, their chaplain, who at this time was detained in Petersburg by sickness. We had scarcely closed the exercises when a deputation came to ask for a service in the afternoon . . . This regiment was in the hottest of the fight at Gettysburg, and proved as fearless in the service of their country as they were ready and respectful in the worship of God."

On another occasion—"I preached in St. Thomas' Church, Orange, and confirmed twenty-three, twenty-one of whom belonged to the army and embraced all ranks from that of general to the honorable post of private soldier. . . . The next evening at Hanover Junction (Doswell) in the spacious chapel which the soldiers of the Maryland regiment had built and ornamented with their own hands, a scene of similar interest occurred. Although the night was very inclement the house was completely filled. By the aid of the Camp and Navy Prayer Book, recently published by our Diocesan Missionary Society, the entire evening service was conducted, with good responses, and the anthems chanted by their own choir. The woods were rendered vocal by their manly voices. I preached there to sons, to whose parents I had ministered in another Diocese, and confirmed eight, some of them members of families connected with the only two congregations with which I have been parochially associated (Frederick and Baltimore).

"Feb. 17. By written request I preached in Libby Prison, which I had been in the habit of visiting to render such services as might be proper, with special reference to those inmates who had been commended to my attention by their friends in the North. I will only state that every facility of access and ministration was afforded by our authorities, and that if all prisons had been as humanely managed neither government would have just cause for complaint.

". . . I preached in the chapel of Upper and Lower Brandon to the servants of the two plantations for whose use it was built. This is but one of several similar houses of worship erected by the proprietors of large estates on James River for the religious improvement of their servants, and where, on my visitations, I have had the privilege of ministering to them in the Gospel. It is sad to have to record that at Lower Brandon, where their temporal comforts and spiritual interests were cared for with generous Christian solicitude, a recent raiding party of the enemy spared neither their little property nor their persons. Those who could not save themselves by flight or concealment were hurried off to find by bitter experience that the tender mercies of their professed liberators are cruel, and that the promised freedom is but squalid poverty, loathsome disease and premature death. The unpretending chapel is left desolate, without a worshiper."

When General Early invaded Maryland from the Valley in the summer of 1864 the Bishop seized the opportunity to visit the churches in the lower Valley counties. At Charles Town, "as we approached we learned that the Federal forces were then entering the town." Leaving it on his right he pressed on to Shepherdstown, which was approached with some anxiety. It was found to be in possession of a handful of Confederates with the Union forces in large numbers but a few miles distant and expected to advance. Though liable to astute and prolonged detention, 'the bell was rung and the congregation assembled. Rev. Mr. Jones read prayers. Whilst I was preaching a note was handed the rector informing him that the Federal forces were approaching. I was not willing to leave the church without confirming those who were desirous to ratify their baptismal vows. Descending to the chapel and calling them about me I administered the Apostolic rite to ten persons." Happily he escaped by a roundabout road, but a few days later, at the parsonage near Millwood, "we unexpectedly found ourselves within the enemy's lines, and they carried off the horse, which, a fortnight before, I had purchased in Winchester to enable me to make these visitations." But Mr. Burwell of Carter's Hall loaned him another which he rode throughout the remainder of his tour and to his distant home in Halifax.

"Dec. 11. (1864). I preached in the chapel of Gen.

Stuart's brigade and confirmed four. In the afternoon I preached in a spacious barn near Port Walthall Junction and confirmed thirteen. The next day I preached in the chapel of Gen. Corse's brigade and confirmed sixteen." This was his last service for the army. For the next three months he was seriously ill in Halifax county.

Bishop Meade and Bishop Johns did not rush to the organization meeting at Montgomery, Alabama, in 1861, but they did attend the October 1861 meeting at Columbia, South Carolina, which was presided over and dominated by Bishop Meade. Bishop Johns took no vehement part in the attempted schism, so he was the natural leader when it came time to revive the Protestant Episcopal Church. Did a dozen bishops have the right to change a Church in which they had been consecrated?

Possibly the Confederate attempted schism was not much more than a change in the printing of one word, that is, "Confederate" for "United." In March, 1862, at Richmond, Virginia, Bishops Meade, Johns and Elliott consecrated Rev. Richard Hooker Wilmer, of Virginia, as Bishop of Alabama, and no other Confederate Bishop was consecrated during the Civil War. Bishop Johns attended and read the gospel at the second and last General Council of the Church of the Confederate States, at Augusta, Georgia, on November 8, 1865.

Due to lack of printers in the South the regular Prayer Book was used by all seven dioceses with the word "United" orally changed to "Confederate," and the people prayed for the President of the Confederated States. Both the "Randolph" and the "Cotton" Confederate Prayer Book, by some error made by the printer

CIVIL WAR!

52a

BOMBARDMENT OF FORT SUMTER, APRIL 12, 1861

Confederate Leaders

JEFFERSON DAVIS   JOSEPH E. JOHNSTON   P. G. T. BEAUREGARD

J. B. MAGRUDER   A. P. HILL   GEORGE E. PICKETT

JOHN S. MOSBY   JUBAL A. EARLY   BENJAMIN HUGER

BRAXTON BRAGG   SAMUEL JONES   JOHN H. MAFFITT

Castle Thunder, Richmond, Where U. S. Prisoners Were Confined

in London, only changed the word "United" to "Confederate" in three places. Other prayer books were printed later, especially for the soldiers and sailors.

A Richmond, Virginia, bookseller, named Randolph, in 1863, employed Bishop Johns' nephew, the Rev. Dr. Kensey Johns Stewart, a Confederate Army Chaplain, who had married Hannah Lee, first cousin of General Robert E. Lee, to journey to London to have the London printer, who had for many years been printing the Prayer Book and had the page plates, print The Confederate Prayer Book. Very few copies of The Confederate Prayer Book ever reached the South, so Mr. Randolph lost the thousand dollars in gold that Dr. Stewart had carried to London. The five bales of cotton sent to London by five North Carolina churches fared better but produced very few "Cotton" Prayer Books.

The Rev. Dr. G. MacLaren Brydon, writing for the *Historical Magazine of The Protestant Episcopal Church* explains that the "Rev. Kensey J. Stewart, D.D., a native of Newcastle, Delaware, was ordained deacon by Bishop Moore, of Virginia, in 1839, and advanced to the priesthood in 1841 by Bishop Whittingham, of Maryland," but remember, Delaware had a Bishop by 1841. He ". . . served as a chaplain in the Confederate Army . . . and died in Richmond, Virginia, June 10, 1902, aged 86 years."

Dr. Brydon continues: "Refusing to concede the right of a state to secede, they (the Federals) refused also to concede the right of the Episcopal Church in any seceded state to withdraw from the Protestant Episcopal Church in the United States of America . . . There are three known cases in Virginia in which the Episcopal minister was actually arrested and taken to a concentration camp for refusal to use the prayer. The Rev. Mr. Kensey Johns Stewart, when officiating in St. Paul's Church, Alexandria, attempted to hold a service without praying *for either president* (italics added by me for emphasis) . . . he was arrested in his chancel, and marched wearing his vestments through the streets to a place of detention." What the clergy did in Virginia was under the control of Bishop Johns, and no doubt Bishop Johns' first objective was to keep his Churches open—and, I submit, neutral, by omitting the prayer *"for either president."* Bishop Meade during the first two years of the War, in so far as his strength permitted, had been a Patrick Henry in the intensity of his patriotism to the Confederacy but Bishop Johns was a humble and tactful Christian servant of the Lord's troubled Church in Virginia.

The Journal of the Diocese of Virginia, 1865, records that Bishop Johns declared the *Army and Navy Prayer Book,* of 1864, "in form and size suited to the use of those for whom it is specially designed, capable of being carried in the side pocket of the soldier without encumbrance, and constituting his valuable *vade mecum* on every march."

In 1861, Mrs. McGuire wrote: "Today I received a copy of *Headly Vicars,* abridged for the camp, by my friend Miss Julia Johns."

On July 24, 1864, amidst cannonading on all sides of the besieged City of Richmond, Bishop Johns' grandson was born. They named him John Johns, Jr. He died in 1922, I believe in California, leaving no children.

Dr. Pennington tells us that Bishops Johns and Elliott risked their lives in their zeal to minister to and comfort the soldiers. On pages 374-376, of *Historical Magazine,* issue of December, 1948, it is related that "Bishop Johns passed some time at the headquarters of General Lee (June 3), discussing the religious improvement of the Army of Northern Virginia. He was impressed by the 'life and influence of this Christian General, and other eminent officers, his worthy associates.' Bishop Johns' diary showed great activity among the men of the armed forces; . . ."

Dr. Pennington continues: "At each council meeting men awaited with eagerness the address of Bishop Johns, telling of his visitations and experiences as he traveled as widely as possible through his extended diocese. At one meeting he told of a letter received from a clergyman, the rector of the parish in Wheeling, asking permission for the rector to invite the bishop of Ohio to visit his parish for confirmation. To which Bishop Johns replied that he stood ready himself to visit Wheeling for that purpose, . . ."

Dr. Brydon wrote: "Money was, of course, plentiful, as inflated money always is; and the people gave generously of it for all Church purposes, to the Bishop's Fund as well as to the Diocesan Missionary Society. For the first and only time in the long history of the Church in Virginia, the salary of the bishop was fixed in 1864 at $10,000.00, payable, of course, in Confederate money. But salt was selling at fifty cents a pound, and other things in like proportion.

"But the people of the Church found a real source of

strength in the fact that all were suffering together. The pastor had no salary because the people had no money; but they could share provisions and food crops of every kind, and patched clothing was accepted generally in all social functions. Immediate offers of aid for the clergy came to Bishop Johns from the Domestic Committee of the Domestic and Foreign Missionary Society and from the Bishop of New York, just as soon as the war ended; but Bishop Johns declined to accept these offers on the ground that it was better for the clergy to be in the same case with their parishioners and share privations with them rather than receive aid from outside. The diocesan council formally approved this stand of their bishop.

"The bishop had adopted the same policy in his own family before the war closed. One of the clergy, rector of a parish within the war-torn and disputed area of the Shenandoah Valley, who previous to the war had business and social connections with merchants and families in Baltimore, found opportunity from time to time to smuggle supplies of medicine and clothing and other necessities through the lines, for a good many of his neighbors. Knowing the needs of the members of the bishop's family, he had offered to secure much needed clothing, but the bishop declined the offer.

"Within a year or two after the close of the war, and following the cordial welcome given to the Southern bishops and deputies as they returned to the General Convention, Bishop Johns changed his attitude, and with the approval of the diocesan council accepted the offer of the Domestic Committee to pay the salaries of certain missionaries in Virginia's rural parishes. Many and generous gifts were made also by individuals and groups in Northern cities for the rehabilitation of church buildings which had been desecrated and made unusable by military occupancy.

" 'Council Journal, 1867, pp. 30, 31. Bishop Johns reported in his address to that council his visit to New York during the preceding year, to a meeting of the Evangelical Knowledge Society, and a meeting of the House of Bishops, and commented on the cordiality of the welcome given him . . .'

"Bishop Johns had confirmed unusually large numbers of soldiers during the later years of the war. But the losses by death had been very heavy. Greater even than that was scattering due to the removal of parishioners as refugees from the war areas, and the removals caused by the necessity of changed conditions. But even as the diocese took note of its losses, it girded itself to meet the new conditions, and began again to grow.

"In his council address in 1865, Bishop Johns had already started the fight for return. He said in part: 'If the endeavor to present a correct view of our position and of the policy which it suggests, reveals the inclination it has given to my own judgment, it has but done what I have no desire to avoid. I trust it has been effected without even the appearance of presumption, or a word that would produce any other excitement than such as is inseparable from a subject of paramount interest. In its treatment little skill or power would be needed to reanimate and inflame those violent passions which have been aroused by the occurrences of the past four years. The tempest might readily be reproduced by a simple recital of wrong and suffering which have been endured. These indeed may not soon or easily be forgotten, nor is this required, but they may and must be forgiven. To perpetuate their disturbing force by vividly picturing to ourselves and others their severity, may serve the purpose of selfish wreckers . . . Christians are to be peacemakers. Their heaven-descended motto is "Peace on earth, good will toward men." In "following after the things which make for peace" as they are commanded, they care not to calculate how long wounded sensibilities may be expected to weep or memory allowed to eliminate their wrongs. The proffered hand may be accepted before the lacerations it has inflicted are healed, or often it would be impossible to do so at all, for there are lacerations which the heart cannot cease to feel till it ceases to beat.' "*

Bishop Meade "the Fighter" died at Richmond, Virginia, on March 14, 1862, and on November 12, 1862 Bishops Johns, Elliott and Atkinson issued a Pastoral Letter which sent "greetings to all the Churches of God whatever may be their aspect toward us politically." In 1865 Bishop Johns calmed an angry audience by quietly saying to them: "Christians are to be peacemakers. Their heaven-descended motto is 'Peace on earth, good will

---

* The Rev. Dr. G. MacLaren Brydon, in 1959, gladly gave me permission to quote from his book *Highlights,* from Dr. Goodwin's articles in the *Virginia Churchman,* of April and May 1923, and from Dr. Goodwin's book *Colonial Churches In Virginia.* Dr. Brydon became Historiographer of the Diocese of Virginia in 1925. He also was the literary executor of Dr. Goodwin.

toward men'." Rebellion To Cleanse A Foul Union was over.

During the Civil War, the Seminary "was in exile." Its faculty and its students were serving Church and State as each thought best. After the War Between the States, Bishop Johns returned from Richmond to assume the leadership in the rebuilding of Church and refounding of the Seminary, "wasted and impoverished by war." In 1923, the Rev. Edward L. Goodwin, D. D., in illustrating the truth of the old axiom, "great occasions give rise to great men," referred to "John Johns and John Cole of Delaware, and others whose names are inseparably connected with the foundation and the character of this School of the Prophets."

". . . in 1868 . . . Bishop Johns was elected professor of pastoral theology." Bishop Johns was "a recognized leader of the 'Low Church,' or Evangelical school of thought in the Church." Between 1816 and 1818 he had taught Hebrew at the Princeton Seminary.

In 1866, the Board of Trustees of the Theological Seminary and High School of the Protestant Episcopal Church, of the Diocese of Virginia, again met at Alexandria, Va., with Bishop Johns presiding as President. Bishop Johns acknowledged receipt of the balance of the legacy from the Estate of John Johns of Baltimore, Maryland, to the P. E. Seminary and High School of Virginia. This was the $15,000 legacy referred to by Bishop Meade in 1859. Dr. Joseph Packard wrote: "The funds of the Seminary, which were in Virginia bank stocks, were entirely lost by the war. It happened providentially that John Johns of Maryland, cousin of

Bishop Johns, had made a bequest to the Seminary just before the war of $15,000, $6,000 of which was found to have been unpaid and to the credit of the Seminary in a bank in Baltimore. With that we started again."

During the Civil War years of 1861-1865, Bishop Johns had lived near Richmond, Virginia, but from 1854 to 1876, except for those disastrous four war years, he lived at the Seminary, at Alexandria, Virginia. By the time Bishop Johns returned to Alexandria, Virginia, the cruel Civil War had almost ruined the South, industries were prostrated, business paralyzed; and "The Church people had suffered more than any other part of the population," so wrote Bishop Beverley D. Tucker, D.D., LL.D., who had served as a private in the Confederate Army. Dr. Brydon relates "that more Episcopal Churches in Virginia were burned to the ground than in any other Southern State."

"Mr. Horace Edwin Hayden . . . says, 'I visited dear Bishop Johns, my cousin' . . ." during the Civil War when the Bishop was trying to obtain Chaplains for the Confederate Army, one of whom was the Rev. Dr. Randolph H. McKim, who, between 1867 and 1875, was the Rector of Christ Church, Alexandria, Virginia, and another Chaplain was Bishop Johns' nephew, the Rev. Kensey Johns Stewart. Bishop Johns was everywhere, always busy serving his people, his Church, his Seminary and the soldiers.

Now we see Bishop Johns through the 1881 memory of the Rev. Dr. Packard, who personally knew and, between 1836 and 1876, saw Johns' good work in Virginia. Dr. Packard sparkles, and becomes transformed

from the comparative to the superlative when he begins
to relate: "No man in our Church has left so fragrant
a memory behind him, not only in our own, but in
other churches. He had uncommon gifts as a preacher,
and might well have been called, as Chrysostom was,
the golden mouthed. A well modulated voice, a graceful
and earnest delivery, a memory which never seemed to
fail him, and a rare fluency of speech, made him very
popular as a preacher."

From the "Reminiscences" of the Rev. William M.
Dame, D.D., a Confederate cannoneer in all the battles
of the army of Northern Virginia, we learn of how
Bishop Johns, then age seventy, had to travel in 1866,
and also of the quality of men whom he helped mold
into fearless Soldiers of the Cross. Dr. Dame wrote, in
the *History of the Seminary In Virginia,* that he (Dame)
left Danville "at midnight, Monday, to reach the Seminary . . . on the following Thursday. We left Richmond
the next afternoon, and caught the boat from Acquia
Creek to Alexandria and Washington (the railroad
from Alexandria to Quantico . . . had not as yet been
built) . . . at Washington, we . . . walked up into the
City . . . amazed by the sight of several hogs wallowing in
a big mudhole in the middle of Seventh Street . . ."

When the War Between Brothers was over, the blare
of bugle no longer ruled man's coming forth to eat,
going forth to fight, and his lying down to sleep or to
die. Generals to privates broke ranks to trudge home, and
one rugged group of dedicated men turned from mud,
axle grease, and camp to answer that supreme Call each
had heard above the crack of rifle, the roar of cannon

and the screams of battle, a Call clearer than that of the strongest bugle blown from a distant mountain to echo and re-echo down the peaceful valleys of life. It was the Call in man's soul that led twenty-five Confederate soldiers to The Seminary to prepare themselves to become Christian Soldiers in the service of one all-merciful God.

That same Call in a soft tender voice forever will speak within young men, calling them to the most challenging and eternally refreshing profession of mankind. That Call I once heard while a student at Harvard but when I shyly, and in a weak spirit of youthful timidity sought the advice of George Herbert Palmer, he, feeling that I was not in earnest, promptly, for the good of the Church, extinguished my advance toward the ministry by advising that I should become a lawyer first and then decide. But that Call is a command, and not something the chosen few can defer to the future.

Dr. Dame, telling of life in Bishop Johns' time, continues: "Every man (twenty-six Seminary students) save one had served as a soldier, in the Confederate Army . . .," and one of those Confederate soldiers was Bishop Johns' cousin, Horace Edwin Hayden; also there were Bishop Dudley, Bishop Peterkin, Bishop Gibson, Ogle Marbury, etc., but those raw recruits, "greenhorns" of 1866, were indeed "a sane and manly type of good men. . . ." They also could play baseball. Dr. Dame says, "we licked that Washington Club 'out of their boots' . . . they were much humiliated because they were 'licked by a lot of preachers,' as they put it."

The pen of Dr. Dame carries us into the many hospitable homes which were clustered about The Seminary: "the homes of Mr. Cassius Lee . . . 'Malvern,' the home of Bishop Johns . . . of Colonel Arthur Herbert . . . 'The Hill' was one big family . . . besides there were, in nearly all of these homes, young ladies . . . walks through the groves with these charming companions were the crowning touch of the social life of our time . . . there were no hard paths anywhere . . . one had to wade in deep and slippery mud . . . living was surely plain . . ." One fellow had a musical instrument, which Dr. Dame identifies as "a sweezy old flageolet." The 1876 codicil to Bishop Johns' 1872 will named Cassius Lee, first cousin of General Robert E. Lee and Arthur Herbert, as his executors.

The Rev. Dr. William Meade Dame, the son of the Rev. George Washington Dame of New Hampshire, was graduated from The Seminary in 1869, and between 1875 and 1878, served as Rector of Christ Church, Alexandria, Virginia. He lived on to 1923, and is described as a man "of singular strength, simplicity and wholesome humanness." The Rev. G. W. Dame's uncle, Jonathan Peter Cushing, also of New Hampshire, became President of Hampden-Sydney College. The chapel window in memory of Bishop Johns was presented in 1908 by Dr. Dame. Many from the North came to Virginia and made a contribution to the cultural and religious life of Virginia. Bishop Frederick D. Goodwin's grandfather was born in Boston, and there were many other Northerners in Virginia.

Yes, living was plain in Bishop Johns' day, yet not too unlike what it was in nearby Montgomery County, Maryland, prior to 1915. We had more bridges, more railroad track, and a few telephones, but we used oil lamps, and very few people could afford the luxury of taking a weekly bath in a hand basin in front of a coal stove in the living room. Whether that Saturday night event was performed over the kitchen stove, or in front of the Kalamazoo living room stove, it took place under the strictest of Victorian rules. In my "modern" rural town, we had mud roads, horses and buggies, but there were no longer any fireplaces, because they went out of style with the advent of the coal, or "chunk" wood stoves, and flue-pots.

Soon after the North took over Alexandria ". . . 'Malvern,' the home of Bishop Johns, was occupied by the Federal officers. His books were sent to the Smithsonian Institution in Washington by some of his friends, but unfortunately with the burning of some of the building of the Institution most of his books were destroyed. . . We were told that Bishop Johns' house and grounds had been but little injured, through the strictness of General Kearny who makes it his headquarters." Between 1861 and 1865, The Seminary was used, abused, and vandalized. Freeman tells us that "Maj. Gen. Philip Kearny was killed when he rode by mistake into Confederate skirmishers," and General Robert E. Lee sent the body of that gallant officer "to the Federals under flag of truce." The military genius and courtesy of Lee knew no bounds.

The Seminary founded foreign missions of the Episcopal Church in China, in Japan, in Africa, in Greece, and in Brazil, many of which occurred while Bishop Johns was the beacon light there on "The Hill." He encouraged the re-opening of Old Pohick Church, "which

General Washington had built near Mt. Vernon and which had been dismantled and used as a stable by Federal troops during the war." Today, people come from all parts of the world to see Old Pohick Church, that thing of beauty; that joy forever. Like the oldest buildings in the Harvard Yard, the proportions of Old Pohick Church are pleasing and simple, and simplicity is the greatest of all art.

You have heard of Bishop Johns from eyewitnesses. Dr. Packard, between 1836 and 1902, also was there, and probably Dr. Packard was the most learned scholar ever to serve as Professor at the Theological Seminary in Virginia. Writes Dr. Grammar, "He (Packard) stepped carefully in the footprints of Bishop Johns, for whose gifts of definition he had a profound admiration, and with whose Princetonian views of man and of the Fall and of grace, he was in close accord." Bishop Johns of Delaware was the most learned scholar ever to serve as Bishop of Virginia.

When the Rev. Randolph H. McKim, about 1916, wrote his biographical essay on Bishop Johns of Virginia, there then were living many men who intimately had known this Christian light of America. McKim and Johns had known one another for about fourteen years, the Bishop's son, the Rev. Dr. Arthur S. Johns, and Dr. McKim, in 1916, were living in Washington, D. C., within a dozen blocks of one another, Dr. McKim for years had known the Bishop's nephew, the Rev. Dr. Kensey Johns Stewart, the Bishop's grandson, John Lane Johns, Secretary of the Diocese of Washington, D. C., and the Bishop's cousin, the Rev. Horace Edwin Hayden, historian

and family genealogist, who had assisted Dr. McKim
in the writing of *The Seminary During the War Between the States* yet Dr. McKim bluntly omitted the
name of Bishop Johns' father. Was this because Dr.
McKim was "seriously embarrassed" by the way Chief
Justice Kensey Johns had disowned and obliterated his
daughter, Henrietta Johns, from her family?

Now, with the passing of more years, the wind and
rain of time have washed the top soil of human detail
from the personal life of John Johns in Delaware, in
Maryland, and in Virginia. But remember, as you read
Dr. McKim's inspiring essay, from Vol. II, pp. 1-8, of
the two volume *History of the Theological Seminary In
Virginia,* that this history contains dozens of beautifully
written human detail biographies. Each presents thoughtful accounts of their respective family backgrounds, and
especially of their parents; that is, its thousand pages
make live again the family background and environment
of every Episcopal Bishop of Virginia, and of other
dioceses, too, except—except whom? Why the family
background of Bishop John Johns—the Virginia Bishop.
Dr. McKim did know the name of the Bishop's father,
Kensey Johns, whose inhuman conduct toward Henrietta
no doubt shaped the course of Bishop Johns' life.

In his book *The Right Reverend Dr. John Johns,* the
Reverend Randolph H. McKim, D.D., LL.D., says: "In
undertaking to give a sketch of Bishop John Johns of
Virginia, who was born in 1796 and died in 1876, we
are seriously embarrassed by the fact that no life of
this eloquent and distinguished prelate has ever been
published, nor does the Library of the Theological Sem-

inary contain any collection of memorial sermons or addresses which must have been delivered at the time of his death.

"The episcopate of Bishop Johns, however, was a notable one. He was consecrated Bishop in 1842 and served as assistant to Bishop Meade until 1862 and as Bishop of Virginia until his death in 1876. He was greatly admired and much beloved in his diocese, while in the Church at large he exercised a wide and impressive influence. Another embarrassing circumstance is presented by the fact that Bishop Johns did not exercise his talents as a writer. The only publication from his pen is the *Memoir of Bishop Meade,* published in 1867 and in this he has absolutely suppressed his own personality. Of occasional sermons and addresses none appear to have survived except those that have been reprinted in whole or in part in the Journals of the Diocese of Virginia. Indeed it was his wish that none of his manuscripts should be published. The best account that the writer of this sketch had been able to find is that given by the Reverend Dr. Joseph Packard in chapter nineteen of his *Recollections of a Long Life.*

"Of Bishop Johns it may be said that he was one of the brightest stars in the firmament of the Virginia Seminary. He selected it as his place of residence in 1854, and there he lived for two and twenty years, up to the day when he entered into his eternal reward, except the four years of the war from 1861 to 1865.

"This, 'The Hill,' was his home for eighteen years, and on that spot shone the steady light of his beautiful life. There he lived and labored, going in and out among the

students and the professors, presiding at the meetings of
the Board of Trustees, worshipping and frequently
preaching in the Seminary Chapel up to the very end of
his life of fourscore years.

"Few men have left such a record as a preacher. For
fifty-seven years he exercised that high and holy office
and for all that long period, from the beginning in 1819
to the end in 1876, he preached Christ and Him crucified,
and this not only with fidelity but with rare unction and
eloquence. He was recognized as an orator of unusual
power. His voice was one of great sweetness and flexi-
bility. His diction was that of a master of the English
language. His delivery was singularly attractive. But
such was his absorption in the supreme aim of the
Christian ministry, such his manifest zeal for the glory of
his Master, that men forgot the orator in the messenger
of God, and went away thinking of the message rather
than the messenger. The elegance of his diction and the
ease and fluency of his utterance did not seem to divert
the thoughts of his listeners from the high theme on
which he was discoursing to the beauty of the discourse
or the personal gifts of the speaker: they served only to
enhance the power and impressiveness of the message,
so completely was the preacher mastered by the gospel
he was preaching. The theme of his sermons was, as I have
intimated, Christ. He seems to have taken St. Paul's words
as the motto of his whole ministry, 'I determined not to
know anything among you save Jesus Christ and Him
crucified.' Whatever his particular subject, it always proceeded from or revolved about the same theme, Christ and
His Cross . . .

Sherman's Brigade at Battle of Sudley Church

68a

BATTLE OF MALVERN HILL

"One far better qualified to judge than I has expressed the opinion that Bishop Johns was a truly great theologian, and more deeply versed than any of his contemporaries in the House of Bishops in the theology of the ancient Fathers. But he never made a display of his learning. Even on the great occasion when he preached the sermon at the opening of the General Convention in Baltimore in 1871, his theme was 'the love of Christ' and he treated his subject with tenderness and feeling and unction, but in simplicity of speech. Trained as he was at the Princeton Theological Seminary, it is not strange that his theology should have shown a tincture of the old Calvinistic masters. Turretin, the famous Swiss theologian, was a favorite author with him. But before all, his theology was the theology of the Cross.

"Yet he could, on occasion, enter the lists with the ablest controversialists without fear of the result of the encounter. Of this we have a striking example in his address to the Virginia Council in 1873, in which he defended the great Swiss Zwingli, Reformer, against the animadversions of Canon Liddon, and Bishop Browne, showing himself a master of theology, and a scholar well equipped at all points. It could be wished that this address might be republished and widely distributed in the Church, both because of its intrinsic merits as a learned and very able discussion of the doctrine of the Lord's Supper, and also because it so admirably reflects the mental gifts, the theological culture and the doctrinal position of Bishop Johns, of whom, though confessedly one of the greatest of the Bishops of Virginia, we have such very scanty literary remains. The writer of the sketch does not hesitate to say that in his opinion it is one of the clearest, most logical, and satisfactory discussions of the doctrine of the Holy Communion with which he is acquainted. It is replete with learning, convincing in its argument, clear and attractive in style. It reveals the fact that, though Bishop Johns was characteristically gentle and gracious in spirit, he was at the same time fearless in maintaining his convictions. It took uncommon courage at that epoch to undertake to vindicate the doctrinal soundness of the views of Zwingli on the Lord's Supper, against such illustrious churchmen as Canon Liddon and Bishop Harold Browne. Yet this Bishop Johns did not shrink from doing. He says, 'Of all the continental reformers, the Swiss leader, Ulrich Zwingli, was most successful in eliminating the errors and superstitions associated with this Sacrament, and maintaining it, in its truth and simplicity, as instituted by Christ.' He then quotes the charges made by the two distinguished authors just named, and says, 'For all this wanton assault, I venture to affirm there is not a pretext to be pleaded.'

"It would be difficult to exaggerate the importance of the influence which he exerted upon the students of the Seminary by the sermons which he preached in the Chapel. They had before them in Bishop Johns a model of what a Christian preacher should aim to be; and one cannot doubt that the graduates of the Virginia Seminary owe much of their success in the pulpit to the high standard constantly before them in the preaching of Bishop Johns. But this was not all. He was also Professor of Pastoral Theology and Homiletics, and the senior class had the rare privilege of receiving instruction from

one who was a model as a pastor, and a master of the art
of preaching. Their sermons were subjected to his
criticism, which, while always kindly, was often caustic
and sometimes severe. The wit and humor which he
mingled with this function, was a great asset to those
who sat in his classroom.

"Of his scholarship in early life the venerable Dr.
Charles Hodge of Princeton Seminary, his lifelong friend,
wrote as follows: 'Johns was always first,—first everywhere and first in everything. His success was largely due
to his conscientious determination always to do his best.
He was thoroughly prepared for every exercise in college
and in the Seminary. Our class had to study Turretin's
System of Theology in Latin. Sometimes a large number
of pages would be given out for examination, and Johns
was the only one of the class who could master them
fully. He was always the best in the class.' When Dr.
Archibald Alexander needed an instructor in Hebrew
in Princeton Seminary he selected young Johns for the
place.

"His episcopate in Virginia, from 1842 to 1876, was
marked by many stirring events, both in Church and State.

"The controversy initiated by the Oxford Tracts was
at its height when he entered on his office as assistant to
the lion-hearted and saintly William Meade. Those
powerful and learned letters of Bishop Hopkins of
Vermont, known under the title *The Novelties Which
Disturb Our Peace,* in which the author, mighty in both
logic and patristic lore, exposed the true character of
the Tractarian Theology as unscriptural and modern and
Roman, rather than Anglican and Primitive—were pub-

lished about this time, and were at once warmly welcomed by the Bishop of Virginia. By his side in this and in the struggles and controversies that followed stood Bishop Johns, always modest and unassuming, but always steadfast and true.

"As to his doctrinal opinions the best descriptive term that we can apply to them is the word 'Evangelical,' meaning by that nothing partisan or narrow, but just the reverse. The doctrine of gratuitous salvation through faith, and the principle of simple trust in Jesus Christ, was, as of the reformation, so of his individual system, the very cornerstone. To it every other opinion was assimilated and by it was squared. If we are actual sinners, verily and indeed, we must be freely forgiven, if God's favor is to be attained at all; and the fitness of a Mediator therefore becomes apparent at once. But as the fitness of a Mediator becomes apparent, so does the necessity of exclusive trust in Him, as being the only link to connect us with the grace of pardon, and the hope of eternal life. He also held to the urgent necessity of the sanctifying grace of God's Holy Spirit by Whom we are drawn to the Father. These two principles, built on the holiness, justice and mercy of God on the one hand, and on the guilt and depravity of man on the other, were foremost in the theology of Bishop Johns.

"As to his churchmanship, he was unwaveringly attached to the Church of his birth. His father, a communicant and warden of the Episcopal Church in New Castle, Delaware, was thoroughly loyal to the Prayer Book and the Articles of Religion which he held to be of the greatest importance as interpretative of the doctrine of the Prayer Book. With the great Hooker he held Episcopacy necessary, not to the being, but to the well-being, of the Church, and gladly grasped the hand of every Christian man as a brother in the faith. He was in sympathy with Bishop Meade and Bishop McIlvaine and Bishop John Henry Hopkins in their repudiation of the characteristic doctrines of the Oxford tracts. But on the other hand when Bishop Cummins raised the standard of secession from the Church, upon grounds which seemed to Bishop Johns wholly insufficient, he stood forth as the firm and uncompromising advocate of loyalty to the Protestant Episcopal Church.

"It goes without saying, after having said this much, that Bishop Johns was a loyal Protestant, holding that the Church of which he was a Bishop should be firm and uncompromising in bearing her witness for the truth as set forth in Holy Scripture and the primitive Fathers of the Church; and at the same time uttering her solemn protest against the perversion of the doctrines of the faith which have been accepted by the Church of Rome for centuries past.

"Firmly but lovingly he sought to restrain that godly man, the Reverend James A. Latane, from leaving the Church; and as firmly and as lovingly would he have resisted the proposal to blot out the word 'Protestant' from the name of the Church. He held strongly to the continuity of our Church with the primitive Church of England, long centuries before the Roman missionaries set foot on the shores of Kent, he also held just as firmly that the Reformation restored the Church to the doctrinal position of the Church of the primitive ages, and that in order to remain Catholic, it was absolutely essential that she should have become and should continue Protestant. He was too well read in the ancient Fathers to entertain any doubt on this subject. He was a thorough-going Protestant, nor did his trumpet ever give an uncertain sound on that question.

"A word should be said of Bishop Johns as a diocesan Bishop. How faithfully he fulfilled the functions of his episcopal office in the visitation of his widely extended diocese—embracing at that time the territory which is now divided into four dioceses—I have no space to tell. It involved long and laborious journeys, often by buggy or carriage, and sometimes in an open boat across the great rivers of the state. 'The care of all the churches,' both ministers and people, rested upon his heart. He brought them on these visitations sympathy and comfort in their trials, ever displaying tenderness and kindness, as well as justice, in dealing with difficulties and complications that must frequently have arisen. He went in and out among the people and the clergy in the spirit of St. John himself.

"My very imperfect sketch would be fatally defective if I omitted to make mention of the fact that Bishop Johns was in the best sense of the word a patriot. He loved his people, and when the great crisis of 1861 arose and the State of Virginia felt compelled in justice to the highest considerations of right and duty to take her stand with her Southern sisters and resist invasion, Bishop Johns did not hesitate for a moment to throw in his lot with the people over whose spiritual interests he had been appointed an overseer. During these four years of terrible trial and stress he was ever ready to give to his people the support of his tender sympathy and his fatherly counsel and advice.

"In bringing this brief sketch of Bishop Johns to a close, I am painfully conscious how inadequate it is to give a just idea of that greatly beloved man of God.

"By his hands I was confirmed in Trinity Church, Staunton, in 1863, and in the same Church ordained in May, 1864. He it was, also, who ordained me to the priesthood in Grace Church, Alexandria, on the 26th of May, 1866, and during eight years of my ministry at Christ Church in that town, I was privileged to enjoy his friendship. The relation between us was thus close and affectionate, and I could wish, for that reason, that circumstances had permitted me to present on these pages a portrait more worthy of my conception of him.

"There are two occasions when his personality shone out with unique and peculiar beauty. One was when he visited a parish for the purpose of Confirmation. His addresses at those times were without exception the most beautiful, and the most impressive I have ever heard. There was an unction and a tenderness in his manner, combined with a fatherly solicitude for those who then entered on the privileges and responsibilities of the Christian life, that I frankly say I have never heard equalled by any Bishop on such an occasion. The members of the class seemed always deeply impressed by his words of counsel, and the whole congregation would be deeply moved, sometimes to tears, as the venerable prophet of God poured fourth his heart in loving and burning words of evangelical fevor.

"The other occasion to which I refer was the annual convention of the Diocese, and especially the closing service. These Virginia Conventions were unique and apart from all others, quite *sui generis*. The sessions lasted from Wednesday morning to Saturday afternoon, whether there was much or little business to be done. Indeed the business part of the Convention was regarded as the least important, and was quite secondary to the frequent religious services and sermons and prayer meetings. These last took place in the early morning, at six or at seven o'clock. Prayers, often extempore, two addresses on personal religion, and hymns filled up the hour, and the Church was generally crowded. The town where the Convention was held presented a beautiful example of Christian unity, Christians of various names uniting in the services, and on the following Sunday all the pulpits would be filled with the Clergy of the Diocese of Virginia.

"It was especially at the closing service that my memory holds the figure of the beloved Bishop Johns. That tender and inspiring hymn, *The Voice of Free Grace,* was always sung and the Bishop always made the parting address with an unction, a tender grace and a spirituality that touched all our hearts. The truth of the Gospel seemed to uplift and inspire him, and the vision of heavenly things, which evidently shone before his eyes, was revealed also to us who loved him. As I look back on those occasions now, through the mists of forty years, I recall the wonderful feeling of brotherly love which bound us all together, and the vibrant tones of the sympathetic

voice of the dear Bishop thrills my heart again and
renews the spiritual exaltation of the hour."

Dr. E. L. Goodwin, in *The Virginia Churchman*,
does give the names of the Bishop's parents and a minor
part of his family background, stressing that "it was a
Maryland family from which he sprang." Sorry, but he
sprang from Delaware Yankees: Kensey and Ann Van
Dyke Johns. Kensey Johns III (1759-1848), had gone
to Delaware in 1780 from West River, Maryland. See: 1
Delaware Chancery, 490.

The Rev. G. MacLaren Brydon, D.D., Historiographer
of the Diocese of Virginia, writing in 1957 of "Bishop
Johns, The Defender and Protector of The Church," and
of Bishop Whittle, who became the fifth Bishop of Virginia upon the death of Bishop Johns in 1876, states
that Bishop Whittle "presents indeed a striking paradox.
He was generally beloved by his people, as Moore, Meade
and Johns had been loved. He was stern and immovable
in his opinions and decisions as was Meade himself; and
he was feared as Meade was feared. Yet . . . no other
Bishop of Virginia has been as steadily and successfully
opposed and defeated as he in matters which stood near
to his heart and his conscience . . .

"In his own mind, he was a tragic failure . . . but . . .
(Bishop Whittle was) a great and glorious Apostle
of the Christian Faith . . . 'when he crossed the River
the trumpet blew on the other side.' "

Bishop Meade also was a great and devoted Apostle
of the Christian Faith; but when he crossed the River,
Saint Peter probably was confronted by an opinionated
and aristrocratic, yet very sincere, child of God, and I

know the clergymen martyrs of the Episcopal Church of Revolutionary Virginia prayed for Meade's admission into Heaven. No one did more for Bishop Meade than did the Virginia Bishop—John Johns.

No one at The Seminary In Virginia wrote a biography of Bishop Johns; because the Seminary was very poor, because the State of Virginia remained smothered by Reconstruction until about 1889, and because the Estate of John Johns, up to 1894, was suing its co-trustee for an accounting of trust assets. The Estate prevailed, in 2 Appeals Cases, D. C., 485 (1894), over its co-trustee, Colonel Arthur Herbert, Sr., who happened to have been the Treasurer of the Board of Trustees of the Theological Seminary In Virginia from 1890 to 1911. The whole atmosphere at the Seminary was not conducive to the writing of the life of Bishop Johns.

To the explanation for the lack of biography may be added three more possible factors. First, there was the tug-of-war between the Seminary and the sovereign State of Virginia over the possession and ownership of the old parish vestry books, which Bishop Meade had spent so much of his time in collecting for his two-volume work on *Old Churches and Families of Virginia.* Second, the State had taken over the College of William and Mary in 1888, so that College hardly could have expended any time or funds in the presentation and perpetuation of its history, of which Bishop Johns had been a vital link. Finally, Bishop Johns was not a Virginian, so, after his death in 1876, he apparently was neglected.

Dr. Charles Hodge, of Princeton Seminary, Bishop Johns' lifelong friend, wrote in 1876, that "Johns was always first—first everywhere and first in everything. His success was largely due to his conscientious determination always to do his best."

Dr. Joseph Packard personally knew that Bishop Johns, from 1836 to 1876, never wrote and consequently never read, a sermon. Dr. Packard believed that in "extraordinary readiness in thought and utterance on all occasions" the Virginia Bishop had no equal "in Congress or at the bar or in the pulpit . . . He never seemed to find any difficulty in expressing himself, and that, too, in the most apt and felicitous words, of which you would not like to change a single one . . . so well trained was his mind and so great and available were his resources."

Dr. Packard further testified that "in Baltimore he was thought the best preacher . . . a new church was built for him, which, large as it was, was filled every Sunday . . . All denominations went to hear him at night . . . He was a Low-Churchman, holding moderate views . . . The last sermon he preached on February 12, 1876," and there he became chilled, "and soon after he had a slight attack of paralysis." On April 5, 1876 "the voice at midnight came" and called him Home.

Bishop Johns took a dim view of biographies, especially those which describe any man "as without fault." He once jokingly said that a certain biographer made his victim out an "old angel." One discerning reader of my manuscript *imagined* she detected a possible fault in Bishop Johns, to which I replied, that Bishop Johns could choose his friends but not his relatives, nor his biographer.

Dr. Packard attests that Bishop Johns' "personal character, his animation in society, his warm and cordial greeting, the indescribable charm of his manner, the bright twinkle of his eye, his playful humor, the culture and bearing of a perfect gentleman, drew all hearts to him. His presence shed sunshine on all around."

Considering transportation of a century ago, it is interesting to note that prior to the opening of the Baltimore and Ohio railroad line between Baltimore, Maryland and Washington, D. C. in 1835, it took more than five hours to make this forty mile journey by stagecoach, at a cost of $3.00 per passenger.

CHAPTER
IV

BISHOP JOHNS
President
College of William and Mary
1849-1854

The President of the College of William and Mary wrote to me in 1959 that "Bishop Johns . . . was undoubtedly one of our more successful Presidents during the 19th century . . .," and Dr. Brydon, the foremost historian of the Episcopal Church of Virginia, added: "Bishop Johns was honored, respected and greatly loved as a great leader all over Virginia." John Johns of Delaware did more for the College of William and Mary than had any Virginia gentleman since the trying days of Bishop Madison, but what manner of place is this College at Williamsburg, Virginia?

Harvard may be the oldest (1636), the greatest, and the richest of all of America's universities, but who would contend that any grouping of Harvard's Presidents, omitting Charles William Eliot, could compare to the College of William and Mary's Presidents Blair, Madison, Johns and Ewell in composite service to God, to country, to education, and to survival of college? Not even Eliot's forty years as President of Harvard can surpass the herculean task performed between 1693 and 1743 by the Rev. James Blair, as the Bishop of London's Royal Commissary of the Established Church and President of the Royal College of William and Mary. What

President of Harvard personally obtained its charter, raised its funds, built its first buildings, assembled its faculty and student body, and patiently and steadfastly nursed it from its bud of babyhood to its bloom of childhood, as did the Reverend James Blair, during his fifty years?

The American Revolution found the College of William and Mary the richest college in America and a generous contributor to Harvard, and left it burnt, poor, and soiled by the "mustard seed" of infidel France. A high price it paid for freedom. Its President, James Madison (1749-1812), First Episcopal Bishop of Virginia, saved the College (1777 to 1812) from destruction. Bravely and with all his life's strength, he strove to rid both College and Williamsburg society of exotic theatrical entertainments, horse racing, gaming, idleness, dissipation, and general depravity of manners, which in part had been created by the presence of French troops and later fanned by the wild Jacobin ideas of Thomas Jefferson. Thomas Jefferson (1743-1826), that desecrator of the Holy Bible and patriot whose Declaration of Independence possibly was a plagiarism from that of Mecklenburg County, North Carolina, or from Rhode Island's prior Declaration, or from John Locke's "Second Essay on Government."

For years after the American Revolution some of the sons of Virginia's best citizens were sent to Harvard, Princeton, and other northern colleges, because their own Alma Mater had become, in the words of Bishop Meade, such a hotbed "of infidelity and wild politics of France." However, honorable Virginia patriots, such

as George Washington, John Marshall, James Monroe,
A. B., William and Mary, 1775, Nicholas, Pendleton,
Randolph, Mason, Bland, General Wood, Col. Harrison,
the Lees, Nelson and others of like depth of decency
stood, like Bishop Madison and Moore, and others of
both Church and College, for true religion and good
morals in America. Dr. Joseph Packard in his *Reminiscences of a Long Life* rightly declared that "Virginia's
statesmen, orators, and educated gentlemen have never
been surpassed elsewhere. William and Mary College
was in its earlier stage of more advanced order than
Harvard. . . ."

Probably it would be more accurate to say that the
"mustard seed of infidel France" did not come into
Virginia until the time of the agonizing French Revolution. Dr. Brydon believes that "the real trouble was not
the presence of French troops in Virginia during the
Yorktown campaign and the following winter but the
great and swelling wave of sympathy with the French
people in the French Revolution of the 1790's that
brought into the cultural life of Virginia the blatant
denials of the Christian faith, and the disgraceful period
of gambling, drinking and dueling that lasted for twenty
years or more."

As to Thomas Jefferson, Dr. Brydon presents this view:
"It was Thomas Jefferson with his English Deism (which
was very different from the French, and which had been
growing in numbers in Virginia as a school of thought,
for twenty years before the Revolution), who did more
than anyone else to wreck the College. He won in cutting
out altogether the Theological Department (The Divin-

ity School) and used its endowment as far as he possibly
could for other schools of the College." Jefferson, who
had received a classical education in William and Mary
College, A.B. 1762, described its beautiful buildings,
designed by Sir Christopher Wren, as "rude, mis-shapen
piles, which, but that they have roofs, would be taken
for brickkilns." Can you feature Sir Christopher Wren
designing "a rude, mis-shapen brickkiln"?

It also must be realized that although Bishop Madison,
A.B. William and Mary, 1772, (a cousin of President
James Madison), unquestionably saved and built up the
college and for twelve years after 1790 did splendid work
for the Church, nevertheless, writes Dr. Brydon, "after
the seizure of the physical property of 'the late Established
Church,' by the State of Virginia under the Act of 1802,
Bishop Madison became more and more discouraged
concerning the possibility of saving the Church, and after
his futile effort in 1805 to secure the election of an
Assistant Bishop he seems to have given up any effort to
administer discipline or exercise any duty as a Bishop,
and the Church went into utter collapse by the time of
his death in 1812." Yes, that is very true, but for some
years prior to 1812 Bishop Madison was a sick man and
probably easily depressed, and even the Rev. William
Meade, who in 1842 became the Third Bishop of Virginia, in his early ministry was weak and timid in his
effort to sense and nourish the potential might of the
then staggering Episcopal Church of Virginia.

Since the Church, the College and the unpleasant
low ebb of morality in Williamsburg were so closely in-
tertwined, mention must be made— even shouted with

THE REV. JOHN JOHNS (1796-1876)
Portrait by J. R. Lambdin, Philadelphia, 1856
Original in Wren Building of the College of William and Mary

PORTRAIT OF REV. JOHN JOHNS (1796-1876)
By unknown artist *Circa* 1820. Original in Wren Building of the
College of William and Mary

joy—to another President of the College, the Rev. Dr. William H. Wilmer. He was the man who should have been made Bishop in 1814. He was the great Christian leader who so valiantly fought for and secured the revival of the Episcopal Church. He was the untiring Churchman who secured a wholesome measure of cleansing reform of the social life of the College and its twin sister, Williamsburg.

After Bishop Madison died in 1812, the Presidency passed to the Rev. Dr. Bracken; then to the first layman President, Dr. Augustine Smith, whom Dr. Swem branded: "a distinct failure who tried his best to move the College to Richmond"; then to the Rev. Dr. William H. Wilmer, and then to the Rev. Dr. Empie, and each in turn did strive to achieve a degree of proper balance between study, wholesome fun, religion, good morals, and discipline. Mr. Thomas Roderick Dew, "a Virginia gentleman, a graduate of the college, and a scholar," as President (1836-46), probably strengthened the finances of the College but stirred up much bitter debate over slavery and the separation of the two races.

Upon the death of Mr. Dew in 1846, the College was run by Professor Saunders and Mr. Benjamin Ewell when, relates Bishop Meade, "by an arrangement with the Episcopal Church of Virginia, the Visitors secured the services of Bishop Johns of Virginia. During the five years of his continuance, notwithstanding the arduous labors of his Episcopal office, he so diligently and wisely conducted the management of the College as to produce a regular increase of the number of students until they had nearly reached the maximum of former years, established a better discipline than perhaps ever before had prevailed in the institution, and attracted more students of divinity to its lectures than had ever been seen there in the memory of any now living." Bishop Meade wrote this appraisal in 1857.

When, in all the history of Harvard, have the President, faculty, and student body laid down their books and shouldered guns to fight for a cause they deemed just, as President Benjamin Stoddert Ewell and all his company of teachers and students did in 1861? In 1865 Bishop John returned to his desecrated Seminary In Virginia at Alexandria, as Colonel Ewell returned to his plundered College of William and Mary at Williamsburg, and thereafter once each year Colonel Ewell rang the college bell to keep alive its honorable charter.

In 1881, dire poverty withered its leaves and rotted its trunk but by 1888 new shoots sprang up. The State of Virginia, for a mere grant of $10,000, had secured possession of the College from its defeated and decadent Trustees and made it a State Teachers' College. In 1906, as a state institution under a Board of Visitors appointed by the Governor of Virginia, it again took its place among America's flourishing forest of mighty colleges, so in sheer determination to survive, it ranks second to none. In 1951, the College of William and Mary took its twenty-second President, Vice Admiral Alvin Duke Chandler, from the nation's mighty fleet at sea to tie its historic cords of the past to the star of an ever rising institution of higher learning.

A scientist, a scholar, a poet, an artist, each can be measured by some tangible creation; but Bishop John

Johns, the savior, defender, and protector of a Church, the President of both a College and a Seminary, statesman, and teacher, only can be measured by those intangible forces of "airy nothing" to which his spirit, his soul, his heart, and his mind, gave purpose, meaning, and harmony. John Johns was not a saint, but truly a humanitarian philosopher.

At the College of William and Mary, I found much interest in John Johns; but that cordial feeling towards one of their nineteenth century Presidents could not extend in factual knowledge far beyond two portraits hanging in their Wren Building, photostats of a few pages from *Colonial Churches in Virginia* and of *Recollections of a Long Life,* Lamb's *Autobiography,* copies of a few sermons, two small paper folders in the Archives of their restful and relaxing library, and some general references in their *Virginia Historical Index,* and *Bibliography of Virginia.* The Wren Building, begun in 1693, was damaged by fire in 1705, 1859 and 1862. I have not located the diary kept by Bishop Johns during the Civil War. The most hospitable Librarian, Mr. James A. Servies, provided me with pictures of their two oil paintings of Bishop Johns and turned each paper over to me with such sincere encouragement that I felt he was anxious and even eager for me to write a biography of John Johns. All that overwhelming encouragement made me wish my labor of love were being done by their competent Dr. Swem. It is a tradition of that College for all to extend friendly, helping hands, even to a complete stranger.

The head of the Biology Department, Dr. Baldwin,

knew the very person for me to see. He laid aside his work, phoned Dr. Earl G. Swem and then personally guided me to the charming home of Dr. and Mrs. Swem. There we were greeted by a man who looked seventy but actually was ninety years old, and who is the foremost authority on the history of Virginia, and of the College of William and Mary in particular. Mrs. Swem served us a "spot" of coffee, and in an instant all of us were old friends.

Dr. Swem, upon learning of the purpose of my call, immediately began telling me about John Johns and I hope I can convey not only his knowledge but some of his interpretative feelings upon President Johns. Some years ago, said Dr. Swem, when new buildings were being erected, he told Dr. J. A. C. Chandler that the College should give some recognition to John Johns, who had done more for the College than any President of his time, and that appraisal began with the Presidency of Bishop Madison. I sensed that had John Johns been a Virginian, he, since the Civil War, would have received greater recognition. Dr. Swem pointedly added "the friends of the College took great pride in having Johns here in 1849-54." Dr. J. A. C. Chandler became President of the College in 1919.

It seemed to me that in Williamsburg there exists a College of William and Mary and a Colonial Williamsburg, Inc., and that the latter may be too northern in its flavoring of history. Dr. Swem agreed with me that the film "Williamsburg: The Story of a Patriot" is not accurate, in that it portrayed women being seen in public places, in Court, and in a mob scene, whereas southern ladies were never seen in such places. Also I doubt if the aristocracy of Colonial Williamsburg were much affected by the Townsend Duty Acts, or the Tea Act, and I also doubt if tea was consumed in Colonial Williamsburg except some modest amount used by the Colonial ladies. Dr. Swem says, "as to tea before the Revolution it was expensive, and not for the people generally as a daily drink." By 1780, many people in the vicinity of Williamsburg were pathetically lacking in both "public virtue and patriotism." Jefferson was there in 1779 as Governor of Virginia.

The glib way "The Story of a Patriot" glosses over Thomas Jefferson's hate of Jesus is an insult to every Christian, not to mention Jefferson's disrespect for George Washington and John Marshall. Dr. Joseph Packard, in his *Recollections of a Long Life,* p. 137, has this to say about Jefferson: "Bishop Meade told me that he had seen Thomas Jefferson in church at Charlottesville. Jefferson always treated ministers with great respect. Dr. Keith once spent a night at his house. I saw in Baltimore, at the home of a Jewish Rabbi, Simon Wolf, two New Testaments from which Jefferson had cut out all the words of Jesus Christ. At Edge Hill Dr. Norton saw the passages that had been cut out." Yet, when President, Jefferson often rode "on horseback with a large prayer-book under his arm," to Christ Church, Navy Yard, Washington, D. C. Some declare that Jefferson eliminated all belief in Jesus and all respect for His authority, yet claimed that he retained his belief in Christian ethics. But in 1820 Jefferson was pleading for the restoration of the "genuine and simple religion of Jesus." Others contend that Jefferson firmly believed that Unitarianism, a crime punishable by death in the early Virginia Colony, would become the religion of America.

Dr. Swem also pointed out that the College was in a terrible condition when Bishop Johns was asked to become President. Dr. Swem added that Mr. Dew had improved the finances of the College but otherwise he had not done very much for it. He was an extreme opponent of the Virginia antislavery men, almost bitter in his public utterances, at a time when the College would have preferred to have been more judicial in its appraisal of the grave issues that led up to the Civil War. Virginia statesmen and Henry Clay were advocating gradual emancipation, with purchase of the slaves by the Federal government. The Brodnax resolution in the Virginia Legislature of 1832 "to abolish slavery was lost by only two votes," wrote Dr. Joseph Packard. Mr. Dew set off an emotional bomb when he, the opponent of the Virginia antislavery men, set out to wreck the highly inhumane and impractical joint effort of the American Colonization Society, the Churches and the National Government to free the slaves and separate the races. Bushrod Washington, A.B. William and Mary, 1778, was the first President of the American Colonization Society and Jefferson had some such noble idea but Jefferson was quick to have his own runaway slaves grabbed and returned to Monticello. Mr. George Fitzhugh of Virginia called the plantation system a "beautiful example of communism." Mr. Dew went wild in his denunciation of the plan for gradual emancipation and found himself caught in the tangled web of sinful slavery when he, as

President of the College, should have directed his efforts toward the attaining of true religion and good morals, such as Bishop Johns did during his tenure in that high office.

Dr. Swem continued: After the death of President Dew, the College experienced such a terrible conflict, caused by a student delivering for Professor Peachy a challenge to a duel over a row growing out of some bitterness over a faculty election, that at first the student was dismissed, and then, says Dr. Swem, the whole faculty was "fired" and "the students left because there were no classes." For almost a year and a half prior to the selection of Bishop Johns the College had been closed, except that one Professor, at his home, gave lectures to a few students.

The Rev. Dr. Edward L. Goodwin, historiographer of the Diocese of Virginia, in 1923 wrote that "after seven years of such highly acceptable services" on behalf of the Diocesan Missionary Society ("above any of our Bishops he was its nursing father") and on behalf of the whole Diocese of Virginia "the name of Bishop Johns had become one to conjure with in Virginia, and in November, 1848, he was elected by the Board of Visitors President of the College of William and Mary and Professor of Moral Philosophy, but at the suggestion of Bishop Johns, Dr. Totten was given the chair of Moral Philosophy" with Bishop Johns giving his full salary to Dr. Totten. "This arrangement continued for five years, during which period the College was practically resuscitated. The matriculates more than doubled . . . he left the institution in a more favorable condition than it had been for many years."

Imagine Bishop Johns serving as President for five years without receiving so much as one dollar, as salary, from the College; and to this day there exists at this College no building named after their great Yankee President, Bishop Johns. Is it because he was not a Virginian?

Thanks to Dr. Earl G. Swem, Librarian Emeritus, College of William and Mary, we know something of what the "exigencies of the College" were prior to the coming of Bishop Johns in 1849, and combining Dr. Swem's learning and Dr. Goodwin's findings with William Lamb's autobiography of 1855, we have perfect corroboration for the appraisal of Bishop Johns, which Bishop Meade wrote in 1857. At a time of bitter chaos and emotional crises among faculty and student body, Bishop Johns provided a "conservative spirit of Christianity." He poured oil on the troubled waters, and restored peace and good order at the College.

Ordinarily the minutes of any Church Convention would be about as interesting as the life cycle of a freckle but not so as to the written record of what transpired at the Conventions of the Episcopal Church in 1847 and 1849. For two years the College of William and Mary actually begged Bishop Johns to become its President. That which you are about to read, from the Library of the College of William and Mary, does more than merely tell you of the pleading that preceded the selection in Virginia, by Virginians, of a non-Virginian, to become President of the College of William and Mary, for here we have in Bishop Johns' own words to the Conventions of 1847 and 1849, the very proof of the considerate, tactful and pleasant manner in which he handled this delicate matter in his Church and grave crisis in the troubled life of America's second oldest college.

(Quotations should be summarized but here my quotations, though long, constitute a bridge erected in printer's ink from the past to the present; from your mind to the mind of Bishop Johns, "so much, no more, no less." I only wish that more of his words had been saved for me to quote.)

"CONVENTION (of the Protestant Episcopal Diocese of Virginia) of 1847.

"Convention met in Christ Church, Winchester, May 19.

"The assistant Bishop in his address laid before the Convention the following statement:

" 'In October last I received an unofficial communication, made for the purpose of ascertaining whether, if elected, I would accept the Presidency of William and Mary College, assuring me at the same time that if it were understood I was disposed to favor the appointment, it would be so made, and urging my consent by various strong considerations, which I need not recite. From my reply to this very interesting communication I take the following extract: "When I consider the nature of the duties of the Episcopal office, and the incessant and increasing demands of a Diocese, so extensive as this, it seems to me that a Bishop in Virginia may not look to any other employment than that of the ministry for which he is specially consecrated. It is from the nature of the case, and under existing circumstances, a mastery incompatible with any second occupation. It would, I fear, only be by robbing it that a second could be served. With these impressions I cannot respond to your suggestions as you desire. Yet so deeply do I feel the responsibility imposed on me by your communication, that I am unwilling to send you a final answer before consulting with my honored associate, in whose judgment and wisdom we all have good cause to repose the greatest confidence. I expect to meet him in Lynchburg on the 13th of this month, when I shall take pleasure in laying your letter before him, and availing myself of his excellent counsel. If his views differ from my own, and the considerations furnished by him produce any change in the opinion which I have expressed, I will then immediately apprize you.''

" 'In the conference which I anticipated, this subject was carefully examined by Bishop Meade and myself, and as nothing appeared that wrought any alteration in my convictions, I found it unnecessary to trouble my correspondent with any further communication.

" 'By others interested in the proposed arrangement, it was again and again earnestly pressed during the past winter. On every such occasion I returned substantially the reply which had been previously made.

" 'In the month of February I was called on by one of the Board of Visitors, who renewed the application, and with great zeal and ability urged my compliance, assuring me that it was greatly desired, and that the Board would make every arrangement as to services and time which might be requisite to prevent any interference with the duties of the Episcopate. His statements did not change my convictions. They did, however, lead me to suspect that perhaps I was too confident in an opinion, from which this gentleman and others, entitled to my highest respect, seemed to differ so decidedly. I therefore thought it but proper to say, that if Bishop Meade and the Convention approved of the proposed arrangement, I should feel it my duty to make the experiment. Not that I supposed it possible to do what I am now performing, and at the same time meet the demands of the new station; but such approval on their part I should regard as an expression of their judgment that I ought to dispense with so much of my present engagements as might be necessary to enable me to enter upon the presidency, with some hope of answering the expectations of my friends. On this statement, the gentleman alluded to replied that he would, with this understanding assume the responsibility of nominating me to the Board.

" 'Subsequent correspondence, with persons most likely to anticipate the probable action of the Convention, led me to the conclusion that the proposed arrangement would not be favorably regarded by the Diocese—that no such general concurrence could be secured as would be necessary to justify the experiment. I, therefore, to prevent all misapprehension, and to avoid even the appearance of any ground of dissatisfaction, immediately addressed to the gentleman alluded to a letter, from which I gave the following extract: "With the knowledge of the fact stated, it might seem to be trifling with the Board of Visitors if I were to acquiesce in your kind purpose to nominate me for the presidency. You must, therefore, permit me to return to the orginal position from which your earnest appeal in some measure moved me."

" 'This letter was laid before the Board at their last meeting, when, as informed by a communication from the Rector, dated February 24th, I was "elected President of William and Mary College and Professor of the Moral Chair with great unanimity."

" 'To this communication I replied as follows: "Under the peculiar circumstances in which I am placed, and in view of the statement which I forwarded to Judge Christian, and which, I understand, he submitted to the Board of Visitors, no action on my part can be expected at present. I conclude, therefore, to wait respectfully for such further information as may place me in a position to dispose of the honorable appointment, without even seeming to be insensible to its importance, or averse from any course which duty may require."

" 'Such, my respected brethren, is a brief history of this transaction, a knowledge of which I supposed it might be important for you to possess, that in the event of its being in any form presented for your consideration, you may be prepared to take such counsel as will best subserve these great interests for the promotion of which we are assembled.'

"The subject was referred to a committee, consisting of the Rev. Messrs. Mann, Sparrow, E. C. McGuire, Hodges, Castleman, and A. Jones, Messrs. Bryan, Nelson, Page, Richard Randolph and Colston. Their report, made on Friday afternoon, was as follows:

"The committee to whom were referred so much of

the report of the assistant Bishop as relates to the Presidency of William and Mary College, have given to that subject the most earnest consideration. They are deeply impressed with the importance of this subject, and therefore trust that, on both sides of this question, a spirit of calm consideration may be displayed, which will give just weight to all reasons which have influenced their minds on this difficult subject. Your committee feel that, under the providence of God, great benefits might result to the Church in Virginia, by placing that venerable and well-endowed institution under such influence as they believe the assistant Bishop would exercise there. They cannot but feel a deep interest in the success of this College, which has conferred such lasting benefits on Virginia and the world, in the education of many of our own ancestors, and many of the most distinguished fathers of the Republic. They are not insensible to the benefits which might accrue to this whole Commonwealth from placing this valuable institution under not only religious but Episcopal influences; and yet your committee sincerely regret to say, that notwithstanding all these desirable results, they are compelled, in view of the great difficulties and serious objections which present themselves, to concur with the assistant Bishop in the opinion that this appointment should be declined. Whilst your committee have come with pain to this conclusion, they feel that some explanations are due to the authorities of William and Mary, and as these can better be made in a full and frank correspondence, than detailed in a report, your committee beg leave to conclude with the following resolution:

"RESOLVED, That the Bishop and assistant Bishop be requested to unite in a letter to the authorities of William and Mary College expressing the thanks of this Convention for the confidence they have manifested in the Episcopal Church of this Diocese, by honoring one of her chief pastors with the highly responsible office of President of that most respected and valued institution; and also to explain to them the objections, in our view insuperable, which compel this Convention, with great regret, to decline advising our assistant Bishop to accept that appointment."

"Pp. 197-200: *A Digest of the Proceedings of the Conventions and Councils in the Diocese of Virginia,* by T. Grayson Dashiell . . . Richmond: Wm. Ellis Jones, 1883."

On December 21, 1848, the Bishop's father, Kensey Johns III (1759-1848), First Chief Justice and afterwards Chancellor of Delaware, died at New Castle, Delaware, and in 1849 the Bishop's oldest son, Dr. Kensey Johns, was in Norfolk, Virginia.

"CONVENTION (of the Protestant Episcopal Diocese of Virginia) of 1849.

"Convention Met in Christ Church, Charlottesville, May, 16th.

"The assistant Bishop laid before the Convention another overture to him from the Visitors of William and Mary College to accept the presidency of the same. In speaking of it, he said:

" 'In the month of November last I received a communication from the Honorable John Tyler, Rector of the Board of Visitors of William and Mary College, informing me that, at their recent meeting in October, they had appointed me President of the College and Professor of Moral Philosophy, to take effect on the first of July next. As immediate action was not required on my part, and as it was now made under circumstances which gave it an aspect very different from that of the overture of 1847, I deemed it my privilege, and but due to the Church in this Diocese, to wait and take their counsel before forming my own decision. My reply to the communication from the Rector, therefore, was as follows:

" 'My relation to the Protestant Episcopal Church in this Diocese is such, that it would not be proper for me to act on this important appointment without first availing myself of the counsel of our Convention. This I will take in May next. If, in the opinion of that body, I ought to accept the office to which the Board of Visitors have called me, I should not feel at liberty to decline the responsible service.

" 'I have recently received another communication from the Rector of the College, enclosing a copy of certain proceedings of the Board of Visitors, to be laid before this Convention, which I now present:

" 'RESOLUTIONS AND ADDRESS of the Board of Visitors of William and Mary College, adopted at a meeting held on Wednesday, the 17th of April, 1849, in the city of Williamsburg, and ordered to be transmitted to the Convention of the Episcopal Church of Virginia through the Right Reverend John Johns, D.D.:

" 'WHEREAS, at a meeting of the Board of Visitors of William and Mary College, in the month of October, 1848, the Right Reverend John Johns was elected to the

Presidency of the same; and, whereas, it is understood that he has determined to refer the question of his acceptance to the Episcopal Convention about to assemble; therefore,

" 'RESOLVED, That this Board transmit, through the President-elect to the Convention, the following expression of their views and wishes, in the hope that it may influence that body to consent, though it should only be for a limited period, to the surrender of such portions of the time of Bishop Johns as the present exigencies of the College demand, and the Episcopal Church may be able to spare, without injury to herself.

" 'The Board of Visitors having regard to the charter and early history of the College, and the religious opinions and ecclesiastical connections of a long line of Presidents and Professors, and desirous to enlist the ministers and members of the Episcopal Church of Virginia more actively in its behalf, have been induced to invite the Right Reverend Bishop Johns to a chief place in its government, confident that his zeal and abilities will render most effectual service in the efforts to place it on the best foundation of which it is capable.

" 'While, however, the Visitors thus invoke the special cooperation of the Episcopal Church of Virginia, they must distinctly declare that they have no wish to make it a sectarian instruction by excluding from the faculty or Visitorial Board suitable persons of other denominations, or by introducing in the instructions delivered to the young anything which can be justly offensive, either to themselves or their parents, in the way of denominational peculiarities. In this respect, they desire and propose to

Four Presidents

Ninth President

Tenth President

Eleventh President

Twelfth President

100a

HARPER'S FERRY IN 1859

Reproduced by permission of Harper and Brothers from *A History of the American People* by Woodrow Wilson

follow the example of many other colleges in our land,
which, though under the predominant influence of some
one denomination, have nevertheless found it to be in
accordance with the dictates of sound wisdom and true
Christian charity to avoid what is controversial and offensive, and to see that only the great, undisputed doctrines
and duties of our holy religion are sought to be enforced
on the pupils thereof.

" 'With the expression of such views, the Visitors cannot but hope that the Convention will see fit to comply
with their earnest desire to obtain the services of Bishop
Johns.

" '(Signed), on behalf of the Visitors,

JOHN TYLER,*

Rector of William and Mary College

" '(A correct copy from the records.)

" 'Wm. M. Moody, Secretary,'

"The preceding statement is, I presume, quite sufficient to put you in possession of the important overture in reference to which I now respectfully ask the
advice of the Convention. If this body decide that the
interests of religion call for our adoption of the proposed
arrangement, and that my Episcopal services can, without
detriment to the Diocese, be so far dispensed with for
the present, as to enable me to devote sufficient time to
the responsible duties of the College, such decision will
control my own opinions and inclinations, and deter-
mine me to accept the appointment and make the experi-

---

* John Tyler, A.B. William and Mary, 1807, was the tenth President of
the United States.

ment. If however, the voice of the Diocese is not decided in favor of the arrangement, I shall be relieved from all anxiety, and feel at liberty to confine myself to my present position and its more congenial duties.

"The Convention, after long debate, gave its consent to the assistant Bishop's acceptance of the position. The vote stood: clergy, ayes 45; laity, ayes 28; negative, clergy 13, laity 15; majority for the measure 45.

"Pp. 203-205: *A Digest of the Proceedings of the Conventions and Councils in the Diocese of Virginia,* by T. Grayson Dashiell . . . Richmond: Wm. Ellis Jones, 1883."

"CONVENTION (of the Protestant Episcopal Diocese of Virginia) of 1850.

"Convention met in St. Paul's Church Alexandria, May 15th.

"The assistant Bishop announced that he had accepted the Presidency of William and Mary College.

"The Convention approved Bishop Johns' connection with William and Mary College and recommended it to the patronage of the Church.

"Pp. 207, 210: *A Digest of the Proceedings of the Conventions and Councils in the Diocese of Virginia,* by T. Grayson Dashiell . . . Richmond: Wm. Ellis Jones, 1883."

In 1849, Bishop Johns, then at Curtis (or Curles) Neck wrote to his wife, Mrs. Margaret (Shaaff) Johns: ". . . To provide for his salary" (that was for the salary of Dr. Silas Totten, Professor of Morals) "I relinquished mine and shall receive nothing for my services but the use of the house and grounds. My support is to be as heretofore from the Church."

Dr. Swem went on to tell me that conditions at the College improved immediately upon the selection of Bishop Johns, chiefly because of his tactful neutrality as to all controversial national issues of the day. More students enrolled than even before and general harmony prevailed among faculty and student body for as long as Johns remained as President. Dr. Swem writes: "I have always thought that he was the one man in a crisis for the College who could restore it with the least friction." And what has the College done in recognition of Bishop Johns?

The 1958 issue of the catalogue of the College of William and Mary erroneously reads: ". . . during the presidency of Thomas Roderick Dew (1836-46)" the College "reached its peak enrollment until comparatively recent times"; however, what is left of the official records of the College, which I found on a sheet of paper in their Library, proves beyond denial that "in 1851 matriculation doubled exceeding by 25 the average since foundation of the College. Number of students in 1853 was 85." This fact is further corroborated by the 1923 statement of Dr. E. L. Goodwin, which I have hereinbefore quoted.

Fortunately William Lamb, a student at the College for one year while Johns was there, wrote during a part of 1855, a diary, called the *Autobiography of William Lamb,* and from this youthful outpouring we are able to obtain a glimpse of some of the highly controversial issues of that time and also see how wholesome the atmosphere of that College had become under the calming influence and magnetic personality of Bishop Johns. Johns stirred inspiration, and hope, and enthusiasm, in the hearts of the students, and a vigorous yearning "for right ever bravely to live," so that each Commencement at the College became an exhilarating launching "on Destiny's sea." Lamb sputters like a gasoline engine not quite properly timed, yet he was warming up to life. He says: "It may be foolish, silly or ridiculous, but I have always felt that I was destined to be prominent in the world; whether for good or evil I do not know. I read this morning an excellent oration by William Wirt, delivered before Rutgers College." The College of William and Mary had done something good for young Lamb. It had stirred his soul. It had started him up the steps of self-reliance. It had transformed him from an adolescent youth to a young man.

Suppose we skim quickly through this autobiography and see life there through the wide-awake eyes of William Lamb, who tells us:

"Hunter Woodis, although a Catholic, spoke before the Democratic Association, at Ashland Hall, in favor of Civil and Religious Liberty." Lamb prepared an oration on John C. Calhoun, that fiery advocate of Nullification and Secession. Lamb writes that he, in 1855, "heard Bishop Johns at Christ Church," Norfolk, Virginia, and "noticed the Bishop had less action than usual in preaching, a decided improvement. The Know-Nothings are holding a Convention here tonight . . ." The students orated over the respective merits of Calhoun and Henry Clay.

Even George Washington was still a subject of debate,

and Lamb, like a lion, roars: ". . . the wretch who wrote the strictures on our Washington is verily too corrupt to be digested in the gut of a cannibal." Of Peter Porcupine's work, and of its "life in the brute Tom Paine," Lamb has this to heave at Thomas Jefferson's pal, Tom Paine: ". . . so base a villain, so detestable a monster, a smuggler, a thief, an inhuman husband, a traitor, a hypocrite, a liar . . . what a concentration of hellish crimes were buried with corrupt infidel Paine. . . ." Lamb continues: "There are two candidates . . . wonder if old Joe Segar will run, poor old coon . . . but by the way this isn't fit for Sunday . . . I go for rendering unto Caesar the things that are Caesar's but they should be rendered up on the weekday and not on the Sabbath. Another Sunday has passed." No doubt young Lamb, in 1855 studying law at the College of William and Mary, derived some inner thrill from sounding off in his Diary.

It was April 18, 1855, and intensely hot in Williamsburg, and alas poor Lamb had spring fever. He groans, "the Judge gave me a long and tedious lecture on Ames' Equity . . . I heard a great outcry . . . I saw the whole town in commotion on account of a fox chase in town, I rushed out and joined in the fun . . . find my law very tough . . . the dreaded fish season is coming in Williamsburg . . . how I hate to hear those miserable fish horns . . ." April, in Williamsburg, can become intensely hot and between fish and heat poor ailing Mrs. Johns must have rejoiced over leaving Williamsburg in 1854. By April 21, 1855, it had turned very cold, and so the weather shifts.

While Bishop Johns was at the College of William

and Mary he found many others like William Lamb, who intensely believed that "the institution of Slavery is of divine appointment," and, continues Lamb, "there are three million of an inferior race held under this institution in the Southern States . . . the idea of amalgamation is as revolting to human nature as it is contrary to the law of God . . ."

Mr. Lamb and I see eye to eye on at least one of his most forthright and accurate declarations: "The Declaration of Independence written by an infidel says, 'all men are born free and equal . . .' this in the declaration is a mere theoretical speculation . . ." But, to return to Bishop Johns. During his presidency, the heat of adolescence was channelled into diaries or let loose in ringing debates that took place between the Phenix Society and the Philomatheans.

It was the custom of that time for people to keep a keg of powder handy. They talked a great deal about the doctrine of States Rights and believed in the doctrine of Nullification, yet realized it was impracticable. Lamb says he does not "suppose it could be resorted to without producing a Revolution." Lamb was a wise young prophet.

Later in April 1855, we learn from Mr. Lamb that Dr. Peachy was back at the College, no doubt due to the wisdom of Bishop Johns, who had a special ability for bringing contestants together in peace and good order. Dr. Peachy calmly terminated a street brawl between a very drunk boy and a Jew. Writes Lamb: "What misery! What horrors arise from 'Rum,'" (yet) "we oppose the Maine liquor law." Later Lamb condemns Stanhope

Burleigh, "the great Know-Nothing Novel . . . gratifying the public appetite for stories and lies against the Catholics . . . 'Uncle Tom' . . . was a finely written romance . . . in no country can Liberty be permanent without the conservative spirit of Christianity." Lamb also was sound in his philosophy.

This bit of Lamb on liquor is rich: "I began to read 'Locke on the Conduct of the Human Understanding.' Went to 'old Bob's' tonight, he was very lofty and grand, having a little more than he could conveniently carry. Mr. Saunders, Col. Garlick, and Mr. Clopton, came to the fair rather tight. . . . Mr. Saunders who is very large and bowing and scraping and the Col. who is very large and Mr. Clopton, who is very thin were grinning at a great rate and jumping and taking off their hats . . . old men acting like monkeys under the exhilarating effects of London Dock."

In a day or two he returned to reading Locke, and confides: "I feel conscious that it improves me . . . I find my extensive knowledge of history invaluable . . . my fondness for history and science of Government shows that I have a natural propensity to be a statesman. . . . Got on a bender today, with Griswold and Perrin first, and then Cyrus Grandy, Hunter and John Murphy, had a glorious time . . . attended Society tonight, heard Randolph deliver a fine oration on the progressive influence of Christianity . . ." Alfred Magill Randolph, advanced to the priesthood by Bishop Johns in 1860, became the first Bishop of Southern Virginia in 1892.

"I went to college today to see a contemplated fight between Sully and Robertson . . . Robertson made a dash

—Sully then drew a pistol and Robertson backed out. The Faculty are in quite an excitement . . . Mr. Ewell called me today to talk the matter over . . . Sully must leave for a month and Robertson for two weeks . . . the affair was brought about by Robertson writing a blasphemous parody on Solomon's Songs and applying it to Sully, which was read in the Philomathean Society . . . The faculty today let both of the fellows off. I regret Robertson was not punished . . . I do long for an opportunity to thrash him soundly."

Lamb paid more attention to college than to girls; in fact he was a very earnest student, although girls were not entirely ruled out of his busy life: "On May the 17th I neglected to state that Miss Mattie Page, and Miss Betty Page, and Miss Julia Thompson arrived . . . old Sheldon Hall seems itself again. Miss Mattie brought me two beautiful roses from Shirley . . . May 23, 1855, the town is in a state of great excitement on the eve of the election." The next day Lamb fears "The miserable Know-Nothings have carried the day . . . the Jacobins are elated . . . the political heart of Williamsburg beats audibly. May 26—Mr. Ewell . . . told me that I had been elected valedictorian by the faculty . . . the first law student to whom the valedictory was ever given . . . Read a long article on the use of tobacco . . . How I love to hear hymns sung in a parlor on a sabbath evening . . . I am a strange being, I love piety . . . yet I do not seem to grow in grace . . . Mr. Ewell and myself had a long talk . . . although the president of an institution of which I am but a student, he treats me as an intimate friend."

Lamb refers to Bishop Johns' special friend: "There

was a party given by Dr. Totten to his Moral and Intellectual Philosophy class . . . the beauty and the fashion of Old Williamsburg was there."

At the July 1855 Commencement, writes Mr. Lamb, "Degrees were then conferred by Mr. Ewell to 5 A.M.'s, 8 L.B.'s, 9 A.B.'s, 4 B.P.'s. Honorary degree of A.M. to Robt. Gatewood and LL.D. to Bishop Johns and Hugh Blair Grigsby. Then followed my valedictory . . . I caused many to weep. Especially Old Buck, or rather Mr. Ewell. . . . I shall never forget it, for it was certainly fun."

I hope you have come to like this nice, normal college man, William Lamb. His pen caught the spirit of his day at College and what an inspiring place the College of William and Mary was in 1855. In two years this fellow had gotten more out of College than most of us carry away after four years. My comparisons with Harvard College are too undeniably true to be branded as out of order. Dr. Packard of Bowdoin College said, "William and Mary College was in its earlier stage of more advanced order than Harvard. . . ." May I add that in five years Bishop Johns had made the College of William and Mary the equal of Harvard? Let me give you the last page of William Lamb's *Autobiography*, because it is so refreshingly American:

"I told all goodby calmly, but when I came to Miss Mattie and Miss Julia, the unbidden tears would steal forth, and kissing them I hurried to the stage. Farewell old Williamsburg, God bless you and yours. Within your venerable walls I have been happy, pleasure has attended me, along your grass grown streets and dear old Sheldon Hall, with those dear ones, 'tis sad to part. My old Alma Mater, farewell. I could not leave these scenes, familiar as the face of some old friend, dear as the memory of buried love with any peace, but a sweet home awaits me, the arms of a Mother, and a happy, merry crowd of little ones with Father and Aunt. . . ."

William Lamb, born in 1835, at Norfolk, Virginia, in his *Autobiography* under date of April 10, 1855, has this to relate as to the birthplace of General Andrew Jackson: "Today while in Father's office on Bank Street I heard Mr. Peter P. Mayo say that Mr. Hodijah Meade," a vestry-man of Raleigh Parish, Grubhill Church, "told him, that he was once staying with General Jackson in Petersburg at the tavern afterwards kept by Powell, and became very intimate with him. Meade told Mayo that Gen. Jackson told him he was not born in South Carolina, but at Jenning's Ordinary, Nottoway County, Virginia; this was before Jackson was spoken of as president. Father stated today that Gen. Jackson was a cousin of Thomas Suffern, Esq., who married my aunt Janet Wilson, and now resides at No. 11, Washington Square, New York." Bassett believed Jackson was born in South Carolina, others insist he was born in North Carolina.

Lamb in his *Diary* makes an impolite distinction between adult Episcopal females, whom he called "Ladies" and adult Methodist females whom he called "women." About 1924 a Harvard Junior from Maryland described his Virginia-born Grandmother as a "lady" and, upon being told to call all females "women," this hot-headed Irishman became enraged and stomped out of Holden Chapel. Soon he received word that he would be dismissed from Harvard if he refused to both apologize to the Professor and concede that his Methodist Grandmother was a "woman." Of course the student elected to be dismissed but to his surprise, he then was invited to return to his classes and the matter by mutual agreement was dropped in silence. It had so happened that President Lowell of Harvard, upon being demanded by the Professor to dismiss the fellow, reprimanded that Yankee Professor for tangling with a Southerner, explaining that this particular Professor, of the Harvard class of 1886, should have realized that respectable white women in the South were "ladies" and not women. I happen to know that the student's grandmother was the wife of Bishop Johns' nephew. No doubt in 1856 most of the students at the College of William and Mary were Episcopalians, and certainly not Methodists.

At the College of William and Mary, Bishop Johns evidenced great adroitness in the management of both faculty and students. It was his faith in Christ and his nice perception in the management of people that enabled him, on two occasions after the Civil War, to save the Episcopal Church of Virginia from self-destruction. It was a combination of faith and tact that crowned with success and glory each mission John Johns undertook from Princeton to his grave.

Southerners, and some of their ministers, were understandably infuriated over secession, tariff and slavery, and the Yankee Abolition Societies did fan the flame of hate but the Episcopal Church, both North and South, firmly believed in the wisdom of separation of Church and State, accepted the "axiom that the Church had no

concern in the affairs of politics," and in no way did
any bishop remotely cause, or bring on, the Civil War
of 1861-1865. However, it was the adroit pro-peace
restraint exhibited by Bishop Johns, before, during, and
after, the Civil War, that probably explains the silent
post-Civil War treatment he so long apparently has received at the College of William and Mary. Bishop
Johns was not a Virginian; even so, in 1957, the Rev.
Dr. G. MacLaren Brydon, D.D., Historiographer of the
Diocese of Virginia, in his *Highlights Along the Road of
The Anglican Church,* declares "Bishop Johns, The Defender and Protector of The Church" in Virginia.

A possible reason for the mild post-Civil War slanting
of treatment of Bishop Johns, the Yankee Bishop of the
Confederacy, is deftly disclosed in Dr. Pennington's
learned article in the December, 1948 issue of *Historical
Magazine of the Protestant Episcopal Church* on "The
Church in the Confederates States." Dr. Pennington, a
native and resident of Alabama, wrote that "The Bishops
of the Southern dioceses at the outbreak of the War Between the States were men of high calibre . . . With the
exception of Bishop Johns, they were all Southern men, of
Southern birth and ancestry; in fact, all were natives of
Virginia and the Carolinas . . ." In Virginia it helps to be
a Virginian.

In Bishop Johns we find a college president who im-
parted to his faculty and students a personal happiness
which flowed from his own emotional health. His own
healthy personality was contagious. He possessed such
refined Christian humility and complete freedom from
hostility, guilt and anxiety, that he did not need to stoop

to compete, thus none became jealous of his wholesome individuality. By closely examining himself and refraining from criticizing others he could become sufficiently detached to collect facts for rational, objective, and acceptable conclusions, so with true independence and deep faith he served both Church and College. His own mental health glowed and became more enriched by the diversity of his varied services to God and to mankind.

On July 6, 1854, after five years as President and Professor of the College of William and Mary, Bishop Johns resigned and moved to "Malvern," a home he had built at the Seminary near Alexandria, Virginia. Mrs. Margaret Johns had been ill for a long time and she no doubt was not physically able to stand any longer the then unhealthy climate at Williamsburg. She died on November 22, 1854, leaving son Arthur Shaaff Johns (1843-1921), eleven years of age, and Bishop Johns surviving her.

The Rev. Dr. Arthur Shaaff Johns, D.D., in 1887, became the Rector of Christ Episcopal Church in Rockville, Maryland, and after 1897 he served as Rector of Christ Church, near the Navy Yard, at 620 G Street, S.E., Washington, D. C. Fifty-some years after 1897 I had the honor of serving on the Vestry of the Christ Episcopal Church, in Rockville, Maryland. In 1959 Mr. Bache Abert, a descendant of Benjamin Franklin and long-time warden of Christ Church in Rockville, Maryland, told me that he remembered Dr. Arthur S. Johns as "an enormous man, over six feet tall, handsome, extremely neat and a very good preacher, the kind who did not read sermons."

Bishop Johns, who died in 1876, willed his manuscripts to his son with directions they never be printed. He was buried at the Episcopal Theological Seminary In Virginia, and those who loved and knew him best placed on his tombstone this terse summary: "He Preached Unto Them Jesus."

As to Chapter IV the author especially wishes to acknowledge the inspiration and helpful suggestions he received from Dr. Earl G. Swem, Mr. James A. Servies, Dr. Brydon, and also from his wife, Peggy Angel Wood, and from Dr. and Mrs. Sumner Wood, Jr., Dr. and Mrs. David Eliab Wood and Miss Peggy Octavia Wood.

CHAPTER

V

Bishop Johns—Bishop Meade

Every true Virginian is very likely to know the name of at least one Bishop of Virginia, and that invariably is Bishop Meade, the Third Bishop of Virginia. In the *History of the Theological Seminary In Virginia,* which places the biography of Bishop Meade ahead of the Second Bishop of Virginia, who, like Bishop Johns, also was a non-Virginian, we read that Bishop Meade "was a Virginian of the Virginians . . . widely known through his prominent family connections . . . essentially an aristocrat . . . peremptory and dominating (in) manner . . .," who, "to the last syllable, spoke the language of the tribe . . ." and suffered from his "godly jealousy for the Church of his fathers." Great stress is placed on Bishop Meade's "high social position," and Dr. Goodwin adds that Bishop Meade "was native and to the manor born" with a reputation for aristocratic "sternness and austerity."

Bishop Meade also was the authority for the story that the Colonial clergy indulged in drinking and all its attendant dissipations to the neglect of their sacred calling, and he wrote "that the church itself was all but abandoned in the disrepute which the conduct of its ministers brought upon the house of God." (Beveridge's *Life of John Marshall,* Vol. 1, p. 23.) Bishop Meade's blanket indictment of about 95 Episcopal clergymen of Virginia, of the Revolutionary War era, most of whom are the

115

unhonored martyrs of the Episcopal Church of Virginia, is pitifully erroneous.

It made my heart sad to find that Bishop Meade, over his seal of authority, made martyrs of the vast majority of the poor, innocent, depressed, downtrodden and helpless clergy of the Episcopal Church in Virginia by shifting to them the responsibility for the near collapse of their Church, as he loudly sang the praises of their persecutors, the great planters of Meade's beloved brand of aristocracy. John Fiske believed that Motley was a historian of the people, and Prescott a historian of Kings and Nobles. Well, Meade, in spite of himself, was the historian whose prejudices and mistakes enable me to retrieve the martyrs of the Episcopal clergy in Virginia from disgrace and oblivion.

"As to Virginia, Bishop Meade, writing in the next century, says that a regard to historic truth forces him to acknowledge that at no time, from its first establishment, was the moral condition of the Church even tolerably good." (Channing, *History of the United States*, Vol II, p. 429.) Was Meade the Bishop, turned historian in 1857, condemning the Church because it was English? Even Dr. E. L. Goodwin admits that Bishop Meade's *Old Churches, Ministers and Families of Virginia* "is ill-arranged, and is by no means free from error or bias." Yes, Meade based his abuse of the martyrs on the highly emotional gossip he in his impressionistic youth had heard from the lips of a few prominent Virginia aristocrats, many of whom probably took out their Revolutionary War-inspired hatred for England on its captive Church and on those of its victimized clergy who

THE RIGHT REVEREND WILLIAM MEADE, D.D.
Third Bishop of Virginia

A little child said she was "a little afraid of Bishop Meade, he seemed so stern and severe."

116a

Three Outstanding Christian Generals

ROBERT E. LEE

T. J. (STONEWALL) JACKSON

☆ ☆ ☆

J. E. B. (JEB) STUART

116b

happened to have prayed and preached peace in lieu of revolt. Did some of Meade's elderly informers, in the heat of patriotic passion, actually, in effect, damn both the Church and its clergy for advocating a return to the teachings of Jesus? Was the American Revolution a disease or could English statesmen and more level-headed Americans have accomplished a still better result through wisdom, time and an abiding faith in all the Church stood for on earth?

Dr. E. L. Goodwin's ardent Biography of Bishop Meade proudly stresses that Meade "to the last syllable spoke the language of the tribe," meaning of "the ruling classes of Virginians." And what manner of thing was the part of that "tribe" of aristocrats of Virginia that snubbed almost seventy-five percent of all the souls of that wealthy colony?

The artificial illusion of Colonial aristocracy in Virginia rested solely on a pride fed on airs of some of the chief planters who set themselves up as privileged individuals. Woodrow Wilson, a Virginian, wrote: "It was only their social weight in the parish vestries . . . that gave them ascendency . . . the chief planters were nowhere greater figures than in the vestries of their own parishes . . . they chose and dismissed and ruled their ministers as they would. . . . Upon the western front of the colony lived sturdy frontiersmen . . ." It was the mountain frontiersmen who forced the removal, in 1779, of the State Capital from Williamsburg to Richmond, and later Bishop Johns moved the seat of his Diocese from Richmond to Alexandria. A wholesome humanitarian spirit did not pervade the Diocese of Virginia during the term of Virginia's aristocratic Bishop Meade.

Bishop Meade's blanket condemnations of the Episcopal Clergy in Virginia, John Fiske, the most authoritative of Harvard historians of the ninteenth century, took with a grain of salt. Fiske questioned Meade's accuracy as a historian, by referring to his babbling against the clergy, as so many "queer stories." Finally, when Fiske had had enough of Meade's brand of history, he, Fiske, concluded: "This testimony against the clergy, it will be observed, comes from a clergyman." Yes, from Bishop Meade, but, concluded Fiske, "it seems clear that the cases cited must have been extreme ones . . ." Dr. Goodwin frankly admits that Bishop Meade often resorted to "data stored in his memory during a period of fifty years." In 1757, a New Jersey clergyman deplored the libeling of the Colonial clergy, and "hoped that some abatement may be fairly made on account of the prejudices of those who relate them," but even so, Bishop Meade in 1857, about a hundred years later, kept right on spreading the blanket libel that the clergy of Colonial and post-Revolutionary War Virginia were wine-guggling, card-playing, fox-hunting, Church-wrecking parsons.

Sir Edmund Andros, after having been run out of Massachusetts, came as Royal Governor to Williamsburg, Virginia, where he promptly picked a quarrel with the Rev. Dr. Blair, the first President of William and Mary College. Andros befriended "Daniel Parke, whose grandson, Daniel Parke Custis, is now remembered as the first husband of Martha Washington." Daniel Parke delighted in such delicate stunts as thrusting a rapier "between the ribs of people who supported the college." On one occasion the "Honorable" Daniel Parke even pulled Mrs. Blair out of her church pew in the presence of the helpless minister, all of which happened in Williamsburg.

Bishop Meade does not mention the fact that the ranks of the "poor whites" were swelled, says Lecky, by "the younger sons of planters, who looked with contempt on manual labor and threw themselves into any military enterprise," because many of them held honest poverty in utter contempt. Burke noted that "slavery diverted men from most peaceful and industrial pursuits." Hildreth wrote that most of the great planters of Virginia usually were heavily in debt and "much more dissipated and extravagant than those of the Northern colonies." Thomas Jefferson was insolvent.

Col. Byrd, of Virginia, in 1733, found the descendants of the Pilgrims to be "frugal and industrious, giving no scandal or bad example . . . by which excellent qualities they had much the advantage of the Southern colony (Va.), who thought their being members of the Established Church sufficient to sanctify very loose and profligate morals. For this reason New England improved much faster than Virginia." (*Westover Manuscripts,* by Byrd.)

Bishop Meade, the historian, while seeking to immortalize some of the ruling class of Colonial Virginia, even charged that the "poor whites" had a flock of illegitimate children. Lecky declared Meade's righteous "great planters . . . a haughty class . . . essentially

aristocratic in their feelings, if not in their manners . . .
resented bitterly the entry during the Revolutionary War
of new families into power." Like the great barons, some
of the great planters wanted freedom, not for all the
people, but only for their Virginia aristocracy. Noah
Webster's *Essays* remind us that Virginia was a great
breeding country for Negroes, and that the concentration
of land and the institution of slavery in the hands of a few
great planters were the causes of "real poverty among
the whites." A yeoman class does not "flourish where
slavery exists."

Bishop Meade, for good measure, added "that the
Negroes of the first families always have considered
themselves a more respectable class, than the poor white
folks." Yes? But it was Thomas Jefferson and some of
the ruling class of Virginia that almost destroyed the
Church. Remember, the Colonial Vestries in Virginia
"chose and dismissed and ruled their ministers as they
would," wrote that learned Virginian, Woodrow Wilson;
and, adds Englishman Lecky in his *American Revolution,* "The management of the colony was chiefly in the
hands of great planters," who probably became patriots
to retain their freedom to set their local taxes and fix
the salaries of the clergymen and, at the same time,
keep their dominating hold on the vestries of their
respective church parishes. Those aristocrats probably
represented less than ten percent of the whole population of Virginia.

In Bishop Meade's monumental two volume work on
Old Churches, Ministers and Families of Virginia, he
in part revels in the glorification of his "prominent

Virginia connections," many of whom, of course, were Episcopalians, which, in Meade's sight, apparently made them a part of the aristocracy of Virginia. The others were "simple folk," or just, as Meade wrote: "poor whites," probably an abbreviation of the well known slang expression: "poor white trash." I remember how white boys used to yell: "Nigger, nigger, never die, blackie face and shiny eye"; and the colored folks would reply: "Shut up, you poor white trash."

All of those ugly inexcusable words were fighting words. I doubt if either Episcopalians or non-Episcopalians liked to be classified as "simple folk," or "poor whites." Obviously Bishop Johns was the more loved by "simple folk," and, by the time of his death in 1876, many Virginians were in that humble, yet honorable, class. Of Bishop Johns, Virginia leaders of the revitalized Episcopal Church of Virginia solemnly, and without reservation, declared: "No man in our Church has left so fragrant a memory behind him, not only in our own, but in other churches." John Johns, a non-Virginian, by his simple, unaffected way of life, had earned the title of THE VIRGINIA BISHOP.

Bishop Meade made martyrs of most of the Episcopal clergy of Virginia during the Colonial and Revolutionary eras. Some really were rascals, but many of the clergy in Virginia were much hated solely because they were Loyalists and Tories in sympathy. Of course "Eminent men associated with the struggle for independence were members of the English Church: Washington, Patrick Henry, Franklin (nominally at any rate), the Morrises, Livingstons, Sterling, Jay, Richard Henry Lee,

Madison, Morgan, the Pendletons, and the Pinckneys.
Bishop Williams once said 'the English Church in the
United States was popularly regarded as a piece of heavy
baggage which the British had left behind them when
they evacuated New York and Boston.' " Franklin
wondered why any minister crossed the ocean to obtain
"the permission of a cross old gentleman at Canterbury"
to become a minister.

Stonewall Jackson, the Christian soldier, told Dr.
Packard that "Bishop Johns had preached for his men
and he had asked him to preach again and said that he
would also be glad to have Bishop Meade preach to
them. Bishop Johns replied that he was afraid for Bishop
Meade to go near Manassas Junction for fear he would
enlist, such was his enthusiasm and patriotism."

Let us re-examine what actually confronted those
Meade-made martyrs. As the tide of revolt against England first licked the shores of Virginia and then slowly
turned to waves of patriotic fervor rolling on over the
mountains and into the valley of the Ohio, those clergymen martyrs of the Established Church of Virginia could
hardly have felt any of the urge of self-defense that could
justify their abandoning their duty to pray for peace.
All were not mere Tories, or Loyalists, but they were
Christian lovers of peace, trying to be peacemakers.

The martyrs of Virginia could not help questioning the
basic motives of some of the patriots on the vestries of
Virginia. The vestries governed the Church, hired and
fired the ministers annually, fixed the salaries of the
Episcopal rectors, levied the taxes, enforced the laws and
even controlled the House of Burgesses, so all power in

Virginia was in effect reposed in vestrymen, many of whom were jealous of their aristocracy and fearful of social reforms. The clergymen martyrs of Virginia could see that many patriots on the vestries were determined not to surrender their power over local taxation, annual elections and salaries of ministers; therefore, the martyrs had cause to doubt if all of their vestrymen patriots were motivated by a deep-seated longing for freedom for all the disfranchised people of Virginia, or merely were determined to retain their long-enjoyed power over taxation, elections and salaries of ministers, without regard to the wishes of either Royal Governor or Commissary. Bishop Meade wrote that "taxation and representation were only other words for support and election of ministers."

The Episcopal clergymen of Virginia were so close to their vestries that they cannot be blamed for having seen the evidence of unchristian selfishness which could have been the basic cause in their sphere of life in Virginia for the American Revolution, yet paradoxically, it was the Congregational ministers of Massachusetts who were fanning the flame of revolt for the sake of freedom from taxation without representation. The Baptists, Presbyterians and Jews also were ardent pro-rebellion. The uniting of the colonies was a mere by-product in which was couched a high concentration of federal government, over which the Civil War against a union was to be fought in years to come. The causes of the American Revolution, as seen by those martyrs, were quite different from the causes seen by the true public-spirited patriots of Virginia, and of every other colony. Of the fifty-six Signers of the Declaration of Independence 34 were

Episcopalians, 13 Congregationalists, 6 Presbyterians, one
Baptist, one Quaker and one Roman Catholic.

Suppose I give you in four hundred words a very
brief review of the basic 1763—to April 19, 1775 causes
of the American Revolution:

Expelling France left the colonies prosperous and England heavily in debt; therefore, King George III
inaugurated a *new colonial policy* designed to raise
revenue by taxing the colonies—taxation without representation brought on the American Revolution. But
remember, Bishop Meade insisted that "taxation and
representation were only other words for support and
election of ministers," in Virginia.

(A) Prime Minister Grenville: The *Sugar Act, 1764;*
currency reform; sent 10,000 soldiers to America; enforced the *Navigation Act* to stop smuggling and break
up colonial trade in lumber, fish, molasses, rum, etc., with
Spanish and French West Indies, and the *Stamp Act* of
1765— a direct tax paid by the masses, on their deeds,
contracts, papers, etc.

American reaction: Denounced by Samuel Adams.
Patrick Henry moved Virginia to disobey the *Stamp Act.*
Nine colonies, at the 1765 *Stamp Act Congress,* declared
their loyalty to the King, denied Parliament's right to
tax without representation and declared a boycott on
British goods. The "Sons of Liberty" stirred up mobs to
enforce a boycott against British trade. Results: Parliament repealed *Stamp Act* in 1766 but passed its *Declaratory Act* maintaining its authority to tax the colonies.

(B) Prime Minister Townshend: *Townshend Duty
Acts* of 1767 on glass, paper, paint, tea, closed New

York assembly; enforced *Navigation Act;* sent General Gage to Boston in 1768, and revived *Writs of Assistance,* paper authority to enter house or warehouse on mere suspicion that it harbored smuggled goods.

American reaction: Boston refused to support British soldiers; the "Boston Massacre" in 1770; Boycott against British goods; John Dickinson's "Letters of a Pennsylvania Farmer" denouncing *Townshend Duty Acts* were widely read.

(C) Prime Minister Lord North, in 1770, repealed *Townshend Duty Acts,* except the *Tea Act.*

American reaction: Samuel Adams and Thomas Jefferson created chain letter, "Committees of Correspondence"; the Boston Tea Party; refused to pay threepence tea tax as did New York, Philadelphia, Wilmington, North Carolina; and at Annapolis the tea mob burned the *Peggy Stewart.*

(D) *Intolerable Acts,* 1773, to punish Boston, closed its port; curtailed freedom to assemble; quartered troops in Boston; and the *Quebec Act* took away Northwest Territory from the Protestant colonies of Massachusetts, New York, Connecticut and Virginia, and gave this land to the Catholic Province of Quebec.

American reaction: First Continental Congress, 1774, united resistance; declared loyalty to King, and *Intolerable Acts* void; formed "American Association" to boycott British goods, enforced by "Sons of Liberty"; wanted peace, rejected Galloway Plan, and agreed to reconvene May 10, 1775.

(E) Massachusetts formed Hancock government and raised an army. Gage fired on "minutemen" at Lexington, tried to capture gunpower at Concord and ran back to Boston on April 19, 1775.

The new 1763 Colonial policy of an insane King had met with reaction, resistance and rebellion.

For some people patriotism is a state of pocketbook. It is sad to relate that in 1780 there was great indifference among the people of the Williamsburg vicinity toward "Public Virtue and Patriotism." (Vol. 1, p. 157, *Life of John Marshall,* by Beveridge.) The martyr clergymen of Virginia knew that loss of power over local taxation and salaries of clergymen was uppermost in the minds of many of their vestrymen.

No sooner was the American Revolution won than did the former colonies begin to fall apart; as some say, the seeds of the Civil War were sown in the Constitutional Convention of 1787, so possibly the martyrs of the Church of Virginia, who prayed for peace instead of war, were right if they believed that a union of jealous colonies in 1776 would but lead on to the Civil War of 1861. Like a chain reaction the causes of the American Revolution, which united the colonies in 1787, set in motion a set of causes for the dissolution of that union in 1861, and amidst that setting of the stage for our second Revolution lived Meade of the influential state of Virginia and Johns of the little state of Delaware, each with distinctly different geographical backgrounds.

Both Meade and Johns were brought up in what I would call the fiery age of secession. A state's right to secede had been a national issue they had heard debated all their respective lives, and, during many years of Meade's life, his prominent aristocratic connections in

Virginia could not have approved of all of the secession threats that preceded the Civil War.* Does Bishop Meade, having been so "intensely patriotic" about destroying the Union in 1861, prove he was confirming the judgment of the martyrs of 1764-1871?

From 1787 (Bishop Meade was born in 1789, and Bishop Johns was born seven years later) to 1861 the pendulum of secession swung back and forth. A patriot Yankee of 1775 became a rebel Yankee in 1804-1814 and a "dam-Yankee" in 1861. The Union could have set the slaves free by purchase and moved them to New England, or into the Northwest Territory, for far less than it cost to set them free by Civil War, and Southern "gentlefolk" could have solved the tariff muddle without having it hurt the "intensely patriotic" great planter class as much as did the Civil War and its "tragic era" of reconstruction. In October of 1861 Bishop Meade "the fighter" rushed off to Columbia, South Carolina, to sever the Church into two parts. In 1865, Johns, standing almost alone, returned to reunite the Church and to be on with the noble objective of preaching unto them Jesus.

At times Bishop Meade had the strong temper of a

---

* Even during the Civil War many Governors of Northern States had no love for a strong Federal Government. The Republican Party of 1860 was in large part the twin of Jefferson's Republican Party of 1800. The contempt for the supreme authority of the Federal Government became so general that a rebellion could have broken out in the North over the Fugitive Slave Act, in which event the South would have fought to save the Union. The theory of secession went haywire—a War To Cleanse The Union was inevitable. Bishop Meade declared there was more justification for the "New Revolution" than there was for the "Old Revolution." Bishop Johns, placing Christianity above rebellion, preached unto them Jesus.

Washington, though more refined as to choice of language, but even that grandest example of American manhood, General Robert E. Lee, occasionally had some temper. Possibly Meade would have bowed to Lee who once said, "When I lose my temper, don't let it make you angry." But "Lee dominated his passions and secured the high temperance and triumphant control" which, as with Bishop Johns, "were among his most marked characteristics." Both Lee and Johns possessed supreme self-control, both possessed uncompromising Christian fortitude, and neither of those devoted friends labored under a drop of haughtiness or aristocratic superiority which detracted so much from Bishop Meade. Both Johns and Lee could lead, and both could follow: Johns followed Meade, and Lee offered to enter the Confederate Army "as a private in a company of cavalry." Both enjoyed absolute freedom from jealousy, self-justification and dominating manner.

Bishop Johns in his *Memoir of Bishop Meade,* relates that "the year 1807 is memorable at Nassau Hall, as the year of the great rebellion, in which"—William Meade —"was so far implicated, that with many others he"— Meade, with one hundred and fifty of two hundred students—"was dismissed from the Institution." After great turmoil William Meade obeyed his "mamma" and gained readmission to Princeton; and these are his words: "An implicit obedience to your will, mamma, I hope ever to consider not as a duty only, but a pleasure."

And he also reported to his widowed mother that bowing to Princeton did go against his sense of honor, and he adds: "I must confess, the finest young men have refused to return. . . ." Bishop Johns concludes: "If he blessed God for giving him such a mother, well might she bless God for giving her such a son."

Virginia aristocracy and prominent family connections helped Meade become a Bishop in Virginia. John Johns, of Delaware, used no part of his aristocratic background as a springboard to leadership in the Church. Meade once was dismissed for the lively part he took in the ugly "Riot of 1807," at Princeton, but would anyone deny that orderly student Johns possessed more innate self-control than did Meade? Do those who condone Meade the rioter, also laugh at another well-born aristocrat, who, in a dining room riot at Harvard, threw the fork that almost put out Prescott's eye? Princeton conferred on John Johns at age thirty-eight, the honorary degree of D.D. Princeton never conferred an honorary degree on Bishop William Meade. The College of William and Mary has had an unbroken chain of Christian presidents, and Bishop John Johns, not Bishop William Meade, is in that human chain. Are not these most compelling reasons why John Johns, by nature, temperament and performance, deserves to be known as THE VIRGINIA BISHOP?

For an approved account of pre-Civil War society one reads in *Southern Folklore,* edited by B. A. Botkin, that "the Episcopal Church is decidedly the 'social' church of the South. The Presbyterians are also acceptable, if less exalted. But the Baptists, Methodists, *et al.,* are, in the old tradition, the churches of the plebeian elements." Bishop Meade called them "simple folk" and "poor whites." To go to Heaven from Virginia did one have to belong to the Episcopal Church or rush into another state to die? Bishop Johns, who was respected by all denominations, was too sensible a prelate to have any part of that silly "well-born" nonsense, or to divide God's children into social classes. The contemporaries of The Virginia Bishop, writing in the *History of The Theological Seminary In Virginia,* certify that Bishop Johns "gladly grasped the hand of every Christian man as a brother in the faith. . . . No man in our Church has left so fragrant a memory behind him, not only in our own, but in other churches."

Bishop Johns emphasized not class distinctions but the very classlessness of Christianity. I imagine that he would agree with Shailer Mathews, who insisted that "The Church must be a minister to society," and not a mere reactionary custodian of pride, power, prejudice, aristocracy and molding doctrine. It was Bishop Johns, in 1857 called "the defender and protector of the Church," who reformed the Episcopal Church of Virginia by completing the transition of the Church from an aristocratic, to a free, humanitarian community of Christians. Meade was "essentially an aristocrat," and it is his type of intensely offensive pride, and lack of humility, which bars the union of all Catholics, Protestants and Eastern Orthodox. Conformity to aristocratic values was Bishop Meade's complex way of life. Conformity to the Prayer Book and Holy Bible was Bishop Johns' simple way of life.

Was it fair, or becoming, for Bishop Meade to weaken his own struggling Church in the eyes of the world? While Meade took off years of his time to write those two volumes, of about nine hundred pages, containing about 6,900 proper names, on *Old Churches,* Bishop Johns attended to the business of being a good example of a builder of the Church and a true Child of God. Would that Bishop Meade had stuck to his calling at a time when the Church needed him the most; but he was a good man, long "subject to nervous troubles," and no doubt got to Heaven in spite of having been "essentially an aristocrat." However, his wailing, negative writings soiled the memory of the martyrs of the Episcopal Church of Virginia. He not only desecrated the martyrs of the Revolutionary clergy but he also often rode roughshod over the poor, living clergy of his own time, so it is fortunate for the Episcopal Church of Virginia that she had Bishop John Johns, a non-Virginian, to bring out the best that was in Bishop Meade, and to pilot a great and good Church of God through the Civil War and on through the "tragic era" of reconstruction.

Bishop Madison, the first Bishop of Virginia, after 1805, "seems to have given up." The spontaneous conduct of Bishop Moore, the second Bishop of Virginia, was not becoming to that of a Bishop: "once while standing on a wharf an Irish porter passing by with a trunk hit against Bishop Moore, who struck him with his umbrella." The Irish often were underdogs in the sight of the "well-born." The "tragic fact" is that no "Bishop of Virginia has been as defeated as" Bishop Whittle. "He was feared as Meade was feared." Even Bishop Meade's staunch admirer, Dr. Sparrow, conceded that Meade "did not always make due allowance for the difference of training, temperament and manners of different classes of people." Those telltale words, from the pens of learned clergymen of the Church, disclose a composite appraisal of Bishops Madison, Moore, Meade and Whittle.

Which one of the five prelates would you select as THE VIRGINIA BISHOP? Looking back through the years of time, we see the five early Bishops of the Episcopal Church in Virginia standing out above the plane of mankind like mountains absorbing their distant horizon. In aptitude, tact and achievement the sustained performance of John Johns makes his mountain peak stand the highest of the five, and thus he becomes THE VIRGINIA BISHOP.

Bishop Johns was so absorbed in serving, so thoughtless of himself, so totally disinterested in recognition, that by his own will he sealed in death all of his own manuscripts. It only was by mere accident that I located, mostly in the (lost) unindexed parts of the *History of The Theological Seminary In Virginia,* testimony of his contemporaries, which reconstructs the mind, the heart, and the soul, of one of the noblest Christian leaders of nineteenth century America. His compact approach to the soul of mankind, in just five words, is cut right there on his own tombstone: "He preached unto them Jesus."

You have read the evidence on how this socially proper son went forth to Princeton from a Delaware home of vested wealth and political power, of how he shed his aristocratic privileges and family connections, and of how, in answer to a mere newspaper advertisement, he descended to the level of honest poverty and remained on the Lord's side all the days of his long life. Into Virginia, Bishop Johns went as a foreigner and,

The Four Bishops of Virginia

The Right Reverend Doctor
JAMES MADISON
First Bishop of Virginia

The Right Reverend Doctor
RICHARD CHANNING MOORE
Second Bishop of Virginia

The Right Reverend Doctor
WILLIAM MEADE
Third Bishop of Virginia

The Right Reverend Doctor
JOHN JOHNS
Fourth Bishop of Virginia

Reproduced by permission of The Protestant Episcopal Theological
Seminary in Virginia

132a

IMMANUEL CHURCH, NEW CASTLE, DEL.

132b

with nought save faith, tact and devoted service, rose to Christian leadership by practicing that which he preached; and "He preached unto them Jesus," stripped of all materialistic aristocracy. You have read the evidence, and now what is your verdict? Is Bishop John Johns THE VIRGINIA BISHOP?

CHAPTER
VI

THE VIRGINIA BISHOP—AN APPRAISAL

The Episcopal clergymen of Virginia, between 1776 and 1790, and even between 1755 and about 1835, were in a wretched position. During the American Revolution, the estimated ninety-five clergymen then in Virginia were under the heel of their Vestries bound by their oath to the Bishop of London, who in turn was under an insane King; swept under the rising tide of revolt against the State and its Church; defeated by Patrick Henry and others in the courts, and hounded, slandered and even mobbed by the Baptists. Many of those ninety-five clergymen are the unhonored martyrs of the Episcopal Church of Virginia.

The separation of Church and State, which gave religious freedom to all Americans, almost brought about the destruction of the Episcopal Church in Virginia, and came close to annihilating its faithful clergy, yet the very patriots who led the American Revolution in most cases made up the Vestries that so often neglected their ministers. The Colonial and post-revolution Vestries in Virginia usually were run by the rich for the rich, which, to a startling extent, meant that the poor were poor because the rich were rich in ownership of the best land. Actually the whole new nation was far from democratic when Washington became President, for seventy-five percent of the white males were not permitted to vote.

Many "aristocrats" of Virginia were offensive and

haughty, and it was the style of the day for them to belong to the Church. That small minority group of hereditary "aristocrats," the landed gentry of Virginia, liked to be thought of as the "gentlefolk" of the upper class. Their badge of privilege was the "periwig," all white and powdered, which many of those lords of the manors delighted in wearing just-so on their often empty heads. The "simple folk" of the lower class were forced by economic necessity to bow very low when many of the plantation owners, with their ladies and their adolescent prigs, entered and left their vested pews in the Churches of Virginia. It took two or more wars, Thomas Jefferson's imported radical influence of the French Revolution, plus the persistent dissenting Baptist and Scotch-Irish Presbyterians to take a little of the aristocratic starch out of the "gentlefolk" shirt of the Episcopal Church of Virginia, and it was John Johns who brought social equality to the Protestant Episcopal Church of Virginia.

But that "well-born" attitude was not confined to Virginia, for even between 1921 and 1925, I found the Episcopal Christ Church of Cambridge, Massachusetts, cold and most inhospitable. I never had heard of an Episcopal Church welcoming the poor until, as a part of my Phillips Brooks House of Harvard social work, I taught Sunday School in an Episcopal Church located in the slum area of Cambridge, Massachusetts; so all Episcopalians in Massachusetts were not "well-born." But here I am wandering from my text, The Virginia Bishop —John Johns, and the hold-over from Colonial times which he found there in Virginia, in 1842.

The Virginia aristocrats, nineteen of them, plus seven

clergymen, one of whom, Dr. William H. Wilmer, should have been named Bishop, picked Bishop Moore, the second Bishop of Virginia, in 1814, possibly because for two years after the death of the kind and long-suffering Bishop Madison, in 1812, they could not agree on a qualified clergyman in Virginia to name Bishop, and even Bishop Moore of New York had previously been appointed Rector of socially correct Monumental Church in Richmond, Virginia, for the pathetic reason that the available clergymen simply were too old, too poor, or too depressed to suit some of the "gentlefolk" of that Vestry. In 1835 Bishop Moore conducted John Marshall's funeral but John Marshall never was an Episcopalian, although, when in Richmond, he attended Monumental Church.

In 1842, the Rev. William Meade, the well-born "aristocrat" of Virginia, at age fifty-three, became the "gentlefolk" Bishop of that state. But, but, but—he, of the "upper-class," was forced by his ill health to hand-pick the Rev. John Johns, age forty-six, of no class stigma, then of Baltimore, Maryland, as his Assistant Bishop. To repeat, Bishop Meade always suffered from his "godly jealousy for the Church of his fathers."

Bishop Meade wrote that in 1812 there were only four to seven Episcopal ministers remaining in Virginia, but, as often was the case, Bishop Meade, when writing as a historian, was in error, because there then were about seventeen clergymen "in more or less active service." Either figure proves that Bishop Moore, in 1814, was a desperately needed recruit, the same as Bishop Johns was in 1842.

It indeed is sad to relate that the Episcopal Church of the Virginia "gentlefolk" caste grew so ineffectual by 1814 that "her ultimate extinction appeared inevitable," and it was not until about 1835 that the Episcopal Convention of Virginia began to show healthy signs of strength and vitality.

Bishop Madison, cousin of President James Madison, and one of John Marshall's professors at William and Mary College, was the first Bishop of Virginia, between 1790 and 1812, then came Bishop Richard Channing Moore, from 1814 until 1842, when the team of Meade, as Bishop, and John Johns, as Assistant Bishop, took over and revived the Protestant Episcopal Church of Virginia. When one examines the political and social realities behind the history of the Episcopal Church in Virginia, one realizes how much it needed John Johns to come in 1842, as a true missionary, to minister unto all the people, whether their economic status was "gentlefolk," or just "simple folk," or "slave folk."

This may be a good time to pause and take a brief look at American transportation during what has been called "The Wonderful Century" of 1815 to 1914. In 1815 the traveller had to use a horse-drawn stage, ox-drawn wagon, wind-propelled sloop and, even as late as 1842, John Johns often had to cross rivers in a rowboat, but I doubt if that bothered him, because, judging from the size of his son and some of Kensey Johns' other descendants, he must have been a huge and physically powerful man. By 1821 there were twelve hundred miles of "McAdam" roads, most of which wound their way westward toward Illinois. The Erie Canal, in 1825, the

Chesapeake and Ohio Canal Company, in which Bishop Johns invested some of his money, and other canals stretched for almost 3,908 miles. In 1836 Dr. Packard travelled by railroad to Camden, N. J., thence by steamer to New Castle, Delaware, thence by railroad to Frenchtown, and thence by steamer to Baltimore, Maryland. "It was the transportation by canal that hastened by twenty years the settlement of the Old Northwest, north of the National Road, that probably determined the collapse of the War for Southern Independence." White immigrants went West by national pike and by canal.

After 1828 the railroads rapidly began to spread their iron rails far and wide, followed shortly after 1844 by the telegraph. In 1844 one could travel from Baltimore, Maryland to New York in about fifteen hours. There was no railroad between Baltimore and Philadelphia in 1844. To be more exact there were 3,000 miles of railroads in 1840, more in Pennsylvania than in all the Southern states put together. In 1835 the railroad between Baltimore and Washington, D. C. was opened. In 1850 there were nine thousand miles with less than one-quarter in the states south of the Potomac and the Ohio.

One of the most unforgettable characters whom I have ever known, was Professor Edward Channing, certainly the greatest of all the outstanding Harvard historians of the early twentieth century. Samuel E. Morison, in *The American Revolution,* written at Christ Church, Oxford, in 1923, declared that Channing, of Harvard, was "the greatest living authority on American history." It seems to me that Channing's appraisal of social evolution in the South is no compliment to the great planter "gentlefolk" caste of Virginia.

Channing, placing fact on fact, came to this conclusion: "of the four hundred and sixty men of highest literary attainment who were born between 1815 and 1850, three hundred and fifty-eight first saw the light of day in the section north of the Potomac and east of the Ohio." I would not care to speculate on how the historians of America would appraise most of the "gentlefolk" of the 1775 to 1842 Vestries of Virginia, and do not forget that Heater declared, that in 1861, less than 10 percent of the white males of the south owned all of the great plantations and most of the slaves. Bishop Johns remained aloof from mere classes, as he ministered alike unto "gentlefolk," "simple folk" and "black folk." He was a Christian servant of God, and not a Confederate or a Federal.

As the Seminary, between 1824 and 1876, spread its wings of mercy, grace and redemption far and wide, as its student body grew into sturdy Christians strong as the mighty oaks that stood like guarding sentinels around their Seminary on The Hill overlooking a nation's adolescent Capital, as generals and their men moved to Mexico on a war of conquest, as Presidents, from Monroe to Hayes, came and went, as the two Compromises of 1820 and 1850 crumbled away and the issues of slavery and tariff split open the English-speaking family of Americans at their Potomac seam, as war extinguished secession, slavery and southern economy, and on through the tragic era of reconstruction, through two violent panics, from stagecoach and canal boat to railroad train, and during a period of vast national growth, we see The Virginia Bishop—John Johns, ever moving out in the midst of his students and his people, and even finding time to serve for five years as President of the College of William and Mary. He was the last of the "horse and buggy Bishops" of the undivided Diocese of Virginia.

From the prime of life, at age forty-six, to age's distant limit of eighty, Bishop Johns of Virginia served God without thought of self, and above class prejudices, while his students carried him in their memories, and on their tongues, to every part of America, and to missions beyond the seas. For one so local in travel his tender influence on men's worshipping hearts spread out from him in all directions like waves on a pool of mercury. His words were repeated, his advice was relayed, his cheering evangelical message was carried to countries near and far, to states, to territories, and to foreign countries, everywhere young Episcopal clergymen from the Seminary in Virginia journeyed on their respective missions of spreading the word of Christ and His Cross. Bishop Johns helped draw mankind nearer to Jesus.

For over fifty-seven years John Johns, the Princeton scholar of Delaware, preached, taught and served God by carrying Christ and His Cross to man. For eighteen years he made The Hill, by Alexandria, Virginia, the headquarters for his good work. His never-tiring feet carried him to every corner of his adopted State and the Diocese of Virginia then stretched from the Atlantic to the Ohio Valley, while his students' feet carried his evangelical message to masses of joyous, sad, troubled and eager Christians—think of the multitude who knew God, the Cross and Jesus, through the heart and soul of this one Bishop of Virginia. He did not dwell in a mansion in Richmond, or on a country estate outside Charlottesville, or on some great landed plantation on the James, but this servant of God dwelt at the Seminary among his students and from there he worked out in all directions among people for most of whom honest poverty was the atmosphere in which tried and true Christians were bred, and reared, and died.

I like to look back at John Johns of Delaware, a believing Christian, a strong, cheerful and brilliant student, first in his class at Princeton, a young fellow with a goal in life, an all-burning desire to become a minister, dashing into the Episcopal ministry to learn its respectful ritual. He cast off his Delaware aristocratic family background to go out into Maryland, and on into Virginia, to "preach the gospel" of Jesus Christ—"so much, no more, no less."

In Frederick Town he lived from 1819 to 1829 among his chosen people. As husband, as father, as preacher he worked, above and beyond the call of duty. On Sundays he acted like a rector and on weekdays he acted like a pastor, yet it was an evangelical pastor who entered the pulpit to preach the gospel, stripped of religious theories and terror, to all classes of men eager to hear more about the Bible, the Cross and Jesus. He spoke on Sundays, as on weekdays, in a spontaneous, friendly, human manner. His sermons were from his heart and not from written pages. His presence and his sermons, with a freshness that moved like a field of Maryland wheat in a gentle breeze, filled his Church every Sunday.

Among his people he travelled on horseback, or by horse and buggy, and often by open boat, or stagecoach, for the railroad had not yet laid its rails into Frederick Town, Maryland. Baltimore reached out and took him to the city where he could do more good because there were more people for him to move among. Twice Maryland almost made him her Bishop. Georgetown, D. C., and Alexandria, Va., frequently saw and liked the man. He was a learned rector but more than that, he was an evangelical pastor who reached and mingled with all of the people of all denominations, and people then, as now, yearned for brave, strong, sober and dedicated men in the pulpit. Then, as now, they wanted warmth, without emotionalism; sincerity that evidenced itself in quiet dignity, without having to be propped up on ritual and trappings, and less emphasis on clerical robes, less religion on the surface of their "gentlefolk" cuffs, less acting of piety, and as Francis Scott Key once pleaded—no cursing, no drinking, no gambling, and more of the simple goodness of Jesus—"so much, no more, no less." Those were Bishop Johns' six most solemn words.

In 1842 this vigorous man's man, who liked nothing more than to be among men, and to be acceptable to men in the sight of God, triumphantly crossed the Potomac in a boat and slowly moved by horse and buggy, or carriage, or stagecoach, to Staunton. Virginians were quick to accept, and keep, this earnest, devoted parson. They could see that at proper times

Johns the scholar was available but his usual way of
life was to be close to all people, the same to all classes
of people, their evangelical missionary, who both
preached the gospel and lived among, not above, his
people while Bishop Meade often tended to take care of
the more delicate needs, and catered to the more refined
tastes, of the more elegant Virginia "gentlefolk" with
their land, their purses, their mortgaged plantations and
their coats of arms. We are told about Bishop Meade's
ancestors and reminded of his "high social position";
and that Bishop Meade was "widely known through his
prominent family connections . . . he was essentially an
aristocrat . . . intensely patriotic. . . ." Yes, and "greatly
feared" and often blind to the refined brutality of many
of the upper-class "gentlefolk."

The Rev. Dr. W. A. R. Goodwin, on the word of
the Rev. Dr. Charles Hodge, a devoted classmate and
close friend of John Johns at Princeton, tells us that
"Johns was a brilliant student at Princeton . . . he was
noted for his eloquence, and for the soundness of his
theology, his sermons being rooted and grounded in
the truth which he had mastered through his long years
of scholarship. He was a man of delightful and contagious humor, and was beloved for his genial com-
panionship, as well as for his fatherly counsel. . . ."
From Princeton to his grave Bishop Johns maintained a
simple course of "perfect naturalness"; consistently well-
managed, well-ordered and at all times in a state of
emotional balance. Johns always was first among his
contemporaries.

I rather imagine that Bishop Meade never was the

well-rounded youth and emotionally happy scholar that Bishop Johns was; never, like Johns, a well-adjusted student in his Class of 1808, at Princeton, so Bishop Meade may have had to conquer himself and, after doing so, he forced himself to lead a life "marked by simplicity and rigid self-denial." Dr. Packard says "there was not a soft chair in his [Meade's] house." Dr. Goodwin says that Bishop Meade's "standard of unworldliness was strict and unbending," yet at Princeton Meade was dismissed for the ugly part he had taken in the "Riot of 1807." Here is how Bishop Johns described Bishop Meade: "When a minister was given to complaining of fatigue from his professional services, he was apt to think the infirmity more moral than physical." Bishop Meade expected his clergy to be miracle men. For twenty years Bishop Johns served under Bishop Meade and had no difficulty in performing up to, and above, Bishop Meade's high, and at times strained, standards of perfection.

Bishop Johns testified that "few things impressed me more during the last days of his" (Bishop Meade's) "life, than his perfect naturalness. In health he habitually thought and acted as if there was but a step between him and death, judgment and eternity." I think that at some point in Bishop Meade's life he put into effect a reformation of himself, and thereafter never relaxed, never let down in his drive for his Church and Seminary. Bishop Meade, called "the lion-hearted," never ceased to be rigidly vigilant but it was Bishop Johns who never varied from a humanitarian course of "perfect naturalness."

I do not know what the phrase "perfect naturalness" meant to Bishop Johns as he applied it to Bishop Meade. Possibly he meant that it was normal for Meade to be a perfectionist, possibly he meant that Bishop Meade had drowned all childhood guilt and adolescent anxiety to exist in a state of rigid self-discipline (after the Princeton "Riot of 1807") but what made Bishop Johns the greatest of all missionary bishops in America was his long-sustained performance in a state of "perfect naturalness" toward all classes of God's children. His life was a long, easy-flowing state of relaxed balance, for he suffered from no repressed instincts and harbored no dammed-up potentialities. To Johns, life never lost its "simple folk" manly meaning of service to God, devoid of self.

One of the dangers of perfectionism is that it leads to unrealistic expectations. I wonder if Bishop Meade, in expecting his clergymen to strive to be saints on earth, failed to heed the warning of the Hebrews: "The law was not given to angels." Martin Luther, in holding out to fallible mankind the hope of salvation by faith, said: "Be therefore a sinner and sin bravely, but all the more have trust and rejoice in Christ who is the victor over sin and death and the world."

For most of thirty-four years this physical giant and intellectual genius, Bishop Johns, travelled throughout the large Diocese of Virginia, which incuded West Virginia, too, and yet from his home port on "The Hill" he found time to teach young ministers how to think, which is the highest function of any Christian minister; for good thinking, coming from God, makes both a pastor and a preacher unlimited in strength. Moreover, Bishop Johns, from the depth of his heart led Episcopal rectors to love and respect all churches, because in Heaven there can be no competing denominations such as we have seen on earth; and who will deny —"Thy will be done on earth as it is in Heaven"? If both the good, but equally archaic, Anglican and Roman Catholic Churches only could realize that the Church of Christ is as broad as Christendom! "Whenever you find the society of the redeemed you find citizens" moving toward the City of God. We are told by his contemporaries that Bishop Johns "gladly grasped the hand of every Christian man as a brother in the faith." That is of the essence of Christian tolerance.

Bishop Johns was seventy-one years old before the Rev. Francis M. Whittle was elected as his Assistant Bishop; and, as Bishop John Johns had worked in harmony with Bishop Meade, that "lion-hearted" and often prejudiced saint of the Church, so, on the high authority of Bishop Tucker, did Bishop Johns work in peace and harmony with Bishop Whittle, who often was most dogmatic and stern. It was Bishop Whittle who refused to consent to the consecration of that greatest of all Episcopal Bishops of America, Bishop Phillips Brooks, of Massachusetts. It was Bishop Whittle who resisted "the separation of West Virginia, and later of Southern Virginia from his Diocese." Bishop Johns was the fourth and last Episcopal Bishop of all of the great state of Virginia. His Diocese of Virginia, which contained 68,797 square miles, is now divided into four separate Dioceses.

Probably the blunt truth is that Bishop Whittle was

so engrossed in seeking to have his own way that he
neglected to write the life of Bishop Johns, as Bishop
Johns so kindly and generously had done for Bishop
Meade. It is rather soul-stirring to see how often it is that
what good men say of other good men unconsciously is
a reflection of themselves. How well can I remember the
general reputation of that beloved servant of God, Dr.
McKim, for he was loved by members of all denominations in Washington, D. C., and Dr. McKim mirrored
his own true soul when he referred to Bishop Johns
as "that greatly beloved man of God."

During the Civil War Bishop Johns remained both
loyal to his chosen people and to the Protestant Episcopal Church. Secession had no place in the Episcopal
Church of America, so probably Bishop Whittle of
Virginia may have been too narrow-minded a Southerner
to undertake an appraisal of non-Virginian Bishop
Johns, whereas Bishop Johns of Delaware simply was
too devoted and loyal a Protestant to believe in section-
alism or cherish the secession of a Church of God. No
Church of God could be broken into two parts over
the Hamiltonian concept of a strong central government,
the selfish sectional issues of tariff and slavery, and the
political theories of nullification and secession. Man
made the Civil War, not God and His Church.

Possibly both Bishop Meade and Bishop Whittle
were too close to the South to view the Protestant Episcopal Church of America as one indivisible church.
The North worshipped money invested in factories and
ships while the South worshipped money invested in
slavery and cotton, and both worshipped false gods, so

KENSEY JOHNS II, 1721-1763
Grandfather of Bishop Johns

148a

SUSANNAH GALLOWAY JOHNS
Grandmother of Bishop Johns

were the basic causes of the Civil War noble? Legalized group murder, called war, is a property disease in total conflict with Christ's being. Did Bishop Meade place the Church of Jesus Christ above the war of man? In 1861, Bishop Meade, swept off his feet, assisted in the division of the Episcopal Church, and declared to Bishop Johns' cousin, the Rev. Horace Edwin Hayden, that— "if I were ten years younger I would shoulder my musket myself." Imagine a Bishop craving to go kill people.

Bishop Johns' philosophy of war stands out in sharp contrast to that of Justice Oliver Wendell Holmes. Bishop Johns believed that—peace is a virtue, and that "Christians are to be peacemakers."

Some cynical soul has written that "Peace is a period of cheating between two periods of fighting," and that reminds me of one chilly day in December 1923, when I heard Justice Oliver Wendell Holmes extol the virtue of war. Both the cynic and Holmes expressed dissenting views, as peace on earth is a virtue.

I had been talking with Justice Holmes in the second-floor library of his brick-row house, at 1720 Eye Street, N.W., Washington, D. C., and when the time came for me to leave, Justice Holmes apologized for not accompanying me to the front door of his home. As he arose from his chair, to bid me goodby, I noticed he was holding one hand to his back obviously in considerable pain. He explained that damp weather made his Civil War wounds ache, and I must have looked very sad, for I had heard so much about the horrors of that war and of how seriously he had been wounded.

I said to Justice Holmes that both slavery and the

Civil War were terrible sins and that I was sorry he
had been wounded. Even though bent over by age and
pain, that once young Captain, almost a foot taller than
I, looked down at me, some sixty years his junior, and in
deep thought, softly replied that the Civil War was
good for America because it molded young men into
a vigorous manhood. Then, pausing for a moment, he
added that the American nation, for like reason, needed
a war every generation.*

Neither Rebel nor "dam Yankee" had ever before given
me any lofty praise for the Civil War. Justice Holmes
had rendered another dissenting opinion.

General Robert E. Lee once wrote: "It is well that
war is so terrible, or else we might grow too fond of it."
Lee was an Episcopalian, "but he had no narrow belief
in the power of rituals or formulas . . . nor dogma or
theology." Said Lee, "My chief concern is to try to be
a humble, sincere Christian myself." Holmes expected
too much of war and too little of Christ. Lee, at Washington College (now Washington and Lee) once re-
marked: "Oh, if I could only know that all the young men
in this college were good Christians, I should have
nothing more to desire." Lee, like Bishop John Johns,
placed his faith in Christ. To them, peace was a Christian
virtue.

I feel that Dr. McKim's biography of Bishop Johns
lacks the color of life, lacks warmth, lacks human interest

---

* Union dead 360,000. Confederates killed in battle or by disease 258,000.
The U. S. News and World Report, for April 17, 1961 © makes this
observation: "If the death rate in World War II had equalled that of the
Civil War, there would have been 3.6 million American dead, instead of
405,000." This corroborates the picture of Confederate agony penned by
Mrs. Judith McGuire, in her *Diary of a Refugee.*

stories, lacks soul-to-soul acts of tender Christian simplicity, but the *History of the Theological Seminary in
Virginia* does tell us of one most heart-stirring family—
the Wilmers. The Rev. Dr. William H. Wilmer, born
in 1782, in Maryland, "one of three brothers, all of
whom entered the ministry . . . ," became President of
the College of William and Mary in 1826. That man's
mother and father must have allowed themselves to be
divinely inspired to have led their three sons into a path
that reached on to Christ's Church.

Dr. W. H. Wilmer's son, Bishop Richard H. Wilmer
of Alabama, was "called the Confederate Bishop, because consecrated during the Civil War." Well, so did
Bishop Johns become a full Bishop in 1862, but what
did Bishop Wilmer do? Did he go upon the battlefields,
kneel by the side of just any dying young man, speak
slowly the Lord's Prayer, and like a mother gently hold
the boy's head, as Jesus, if physically present, would
have done? Dr. Phillips does not tell us, but Dr. Phillips
does tell, from Bishop R. H. Wilmer's lips, of the
deepest act of love I ever have learned of a Bishop
doing.

Remember, I am a "simple folk" Methodist at heart
and I must wander away for just a few lines to tell you
more about the human kindness of the Wilmers. The
Confederate Bishop tells of how his cousin, Bishop Pere
Wilmer, while visiting in New Orleans, went to see a
dying colored man, who had been a Wilmer family
slave when all the Wilmer children were too young to
know any race distinctions. "After praying with him
Bishop Pere Wilmer said 'Joe, is there anything more I

can do . . .?' The old colored man answered: 'Master
Pere, you know, when we were little boys, how we
used to play under the old tree in the garden, and how,
when we were tired, we would sleep in each other's
arms? I think if you would lie by me and hold me in
your arms again, I will die more easily.' Without a
moment's hesitation, the Bishop lay down by the old
colored man and held him in his arms till his soul de-
parted. It was an act of tender, gracious consideration."
No! No! No! Don't call that a mere act of "tender
gracious consideration!" It was a Christ-like act of true
brotherly love. A Bishop had acted on earth as Jesus
would that he should have done.

May I continue to wander for just a few more lines?
How I wish I could bring Bishop Johns back to life by
telling you of some of the simple things he must have
done for others while on earth! Bishop R. H. Wilmer,
of Alabama, had a son, Dr. William Holland Wilmer,
who was the most famous eye specialist in the world.
Even now I can feel his gentle hand on my head and
hear his soft voice comforting my worried Mother,
because I, her most precious possession, had eyes that
crossed. I then was four or five years old. Dr. Wilmer's
contemporary at the Episcopal High School in Virginia, the Rev. Arthur B. Kinsolving, D.D., writing
of Dr. William Holland Wilmer, says, "We remember
him with his studious, painstaking habits, his thorough-
ness in the performance of every task, his high and
serious purpose, and his beautiful love for one of the
noblest fathers that ever man had." Into eternity the

Wilmer Eye Clinic of Johns Hopkins Hospital will memorialize Dr. William Holland Wilmer.

Johns Hopkins University opened in 1876, the year Bishop Johns died. It had been founded by Johns Hopkins (1795-1873), a wealthy Baltimore merchant, who was named after his grandfather Johns Hopkins, and born in Anne Arundel County, Maryland. Richard Johns, the emigrant, married Elizabeth Kensey, and lived at "the Cliffs," Calvert County, Maryland, and their son, Kensey Johns, I (1685-1729), was of Calvert County, and his son Kensey Johns, II (1721-1763), was High Sheriff of Anne Arundel County, Maryland, where Bishop John Johns' father, Chief Justice (afterwards Chancellor) Kensey Johns, III (1759-1848), of "Sudley," West River, Maryland, lived before moving to New Castle, Delaware. Bishop John Johns (1796-1876) and Johns Hopkins (1795-1873), the Baltimore philanthropist, were third cousins.

Obviously Johns, although consecrated Bishop in 1862 at Richmond, Virginia, the Capital of the Confederacy, could not be called the Confederate Bishop, nor was he a Yankee Bishop, because he was The Virginia Bishop. He went South, in 1861, to serve God's children of his Diocese, who then were gripped in a North-South hysteria of hate. As Bishop he held the Cross above the bullets of bitterness, yet his physical person, in and around Richmond, and travelling about in Virginia, was more exposed to the dangers of war than were most of the political Generals—about 7,500—of the North. He got around like the proverbial flea. He was so active that he only could be "tied in Heaven." The Virginia

Bishop was in the thick of the war, in or near a city the capture of which was one of the four major objectives of the Union Army, and there in Virginia he remained to the bitter end, but, like Christ, he took no sides in the War Between The States. Bishop Johns served his Diocese, which happened to have been Virginia.

During the Civil War The Virginia Bishop lived in or near Richmond, Virginia. Quite possibly he had lived near Malvern Hill, where, in July of 1862, the Union forces were held back from the gates of Richmond at a killed and wounded loss of 19,155 Confederate men and 9,796 Union men. From Malvern Hill, amidst stately locust trees and carpeted in velvet green grass, one looked out to dense forests on the far side of the River James, and over that pastoral scene of simple peace came a roar of battle that transformed God's intended peace and beauty into a horrible landscape of cracking rifles, booming cannon, violent death and even more frightful pain *en masse;* and The Virginia Bishop was there where as a servant of God he belonged.

Woodrow Wilson describes this series of battles less vividly than Freeman. Wilson tells of how Stonewall Jackson rushed his soldiers by rail to help General Robert E. Lee. "For seven memorable days the two beat McClellan's army back until Richmond was safe."

Channing writes that "On July 1, the Federal army found itself most advantageously posted on the crest of Malvern Hill . . . Lee attacked again and again, to be repulsed with terrible loss. Had the Union line gone forward on that afternoon, the war might have ended then and there . . . McClellan withdrew . . . Halleck decided to withdraw the Union Army of the Potomac by water from the James . . . the greatest single disaster of the war."

You will recall that in 1854 Bishop Johns built his house at the Episcopal Seminary in Virginia and that home he called "Malvern." In his will he wrote: "To my daughter Julianna Johns I devise Malvern, the Farm on which I reside, containing between fifty and sixty acres. . . ."

All we know from him of a pathetic tone, about his hour to hour, month to month and year to year experiences in, and around, Richmond, and throughout Virginia, is the little he relates in his holographic will of May 29, 1872, that is, one which he penned with his own hand at his home, "Malvern," Fairfax County, Virginia. In that will he gave to Arthur Shaaff Johns, his minister son, "such theological works as I have collected since the total loss of my Library during the War. Also all my Manuscripts, with strict directions that no part of them be printed."

Although Bishop Johns was living at the Seminary, only a few miles from where the first major battle of the Civil War was fought, and living near Richmond when that city was taken, his all-absorbing desire was to hold high the Cross of Jesus before those who suffered, those who died and those who survived in his Diocese. At war's end he hastened back to revive his Church; to re-create and restore the Seminary In Virginia, and to resume his leadership of his Diocese in both Virginias. He was not for glorifying war but for glorifying God by quickly reuniting the Episcopal Church and refounding the Seminary, so young men could move forward as ministers "to preach the gospel" as written in the Scriptures, to the whole war-torn nation.

In 1825 he had insisted that ministerial students coming to the Seminary must be educated men, college graduates or the equivalent in basic knowledge. In 1859, the year in which Bishop Phillips Brooks, A.B. Harvard, 1855, was graduated from the Theological Seminary In Virginia, Bishop Johns looked back over his trusteeship of the Seminary In Virginia and earnestly declared, "that care has been taken that in this school the doctrines of the Protestant Reformation, which are the doctrines of the Scriptures, and of which justification by faith is the keynote, should be taught with distinction and decision; that the ecclesiastical policy inculcated here has been that set forth in the Preface to the Ordination Services—so much, no more, no less, in a word, that the three orders have existed from the Apostles' times, and no other ministry to be recognized 'in this Church.'" To that high goal Bishop Johns restored the Episcopal Church and refounded the Seminary, at the close of the Civil War. Holmes glorified war while Johns glorified the whole Church of Jesus and ordered that the Protestant Episcopal Seminary In Virginia must teach within the limits of the four corners of the Holy Bible—"so much, no more, no less. . . ."

Between 1842 and 1862, Bishop Meade was often ill, or busy writing, so in effect he frequently was Bishop in name only, but Bishop Meade did receive so much praise and credit from his devoted and unselfish Assistant Bishop Johns, that it is often difficult to separate the hidden greatness of the patient, humble and loving Bishop Johns from the credit rightfully due Bishop Meade during those years. Actually Bishop Johns was so extremely meek, constructive and retiring, that his personal power quietly held together and carried on the Church, and the Seminary In Virginia, yet for all of his own accomplishments Bishop Johns gave total credit to Bishop Meade. Bishop Johns' *Life of Bishop Meade* is like a story written by one very gifted and literary brother of his own dearly beloved and deceased older brother. Actually, Bishop Meade, the "lion-hearted," was too intensely patriotic to Virginia to be free from extreme bias, and his two-volume work on the old aristocratic families of Virginia is "too reactionary, ill-arranged and prejudiced" to place him on the same high level of pastoral service as Bishop Johns. It was a young child who innocently and frankly gave the most honest and disarming appraisal of Bishop Meade, when she "confessed that she was a little afraid of him, he seemed so stern and severe." The evidence proves beyond all doubt that Bishop Meade was stern, severe and feared, whereas Bishop Johns, quiet, strong and constraining, was gentle, kind and beloved by all classes of people.

The Rev. Dr. Edward Lewis Goodwin, for many years Historiographer of the Diocese of Virginia, and Editor of the *Southern Churchman,* who personally had known Bishop Johns, declared without qualification that The Virginia Bishop was "the greatest preacher that the

Church In Virginia has ever had . . . a delightful companion . . . always dignified, yet he had a fine sense of humor," and Dr. Goodwin goes on to disclose that Bishop Johns' "influence in the Diocese during the lifetime of Bishop Meade was quiet and unobtrusive as he purposely made it, but it was nonetheless strong and constraining, and he had the love and perfect confidence of all his people." Dr. Brydon advised me that Bishop Johns "did his own work and carried on through the years of Bishop Meade's ill-health." Bishop Meade died in 1862 after twenty years of failing health.

Possibly we may say that between 1842 and 1862 Virginia had two Bishops, one of whom carried on until 1876, and, viewed in that way, Bishop John Johns was Bishop of Virginia from 1842 to 1876, a total of thirty-four years. When presented in his true light, Bishop Johns becomes "The Defender and Protector of the Church," the greatest of all the early Episcopal Bishops of Virginia. His cheerful, confident faith, his simple way of thinking, speaking and living made him the foremost Evangelical leader of America.

While Kensey Johns in pomp moved from law's first Chief Justice, to equity's first Chancellor of Delaware, and by his wealth and political power handed his high rank on, in 1832, to his aristocratic son, Kensey Johns, Jr., two of his democratic sons were moving before the Cross of Jesus, ministering unto the soul of man, to the rich, to the poor, to the high, and to those held down in honest poverty, all, if believers, favorites in the sight of God. What a blunt contrast between the father-made aristocratic path of brother Chancellor Kensey Johns,

Jr., who died in 1857, and the self-made paths of those two Soldiers of the Cross, brothers Rev. Dr. Henry Van Dyke Johns, D.D., who died in 1859, and Rt. Rev. Dr. John Johns, D.D. LL.D., fourth Episcopal Bishop of the State of Virginia, who died in 1876, whispering, "Guide me—wash me—clothe me—help me under the shadow of Thy wings."

This much we do know about The Virginia Bishop; namely, that in the days of his youth he answered the Call of Jesus, and at the end of his life, it was the general and undisputed consensus of learned opinion of his day in America, that Bishop Johns was "more deeply versed than any of his contemporaries in the House of Bishops in the theology of the ancient Fathers . . . a scholar well equipped at all points . . . one of the greatest of the Bishops of Virginia . . . a model of what a Christian preacher should be . . . always modest and unassuming, but always steadfast and true . . . He preached unto them Jesus"—in his six greatest words, "so much, no more, no less"; and, in life, in death, his eyes were focused on—Christ and His Cross.

Lord, with glowing heart, John Johns ever praised Thee, and, subject to Thy will, I take the leave of humbly calling John Johns—*The Virginia Bishop.*

APPENDIX

The "Serious Embarrassment"

Several years ago, while serving on the Vestry of Christ
Episcopal Church, Rockville, Maryland, I had had pointed
out to me a picture of a former Rector of my Church, who
was Bishop Johns' son, the Rev. Dr. Arthur Shaaff Johns
(1843-1921). In 1958 I happened to ask one of my aunts
if she remembered Rev. Arthur Shaaff Johns, and, being more
outspoken than had been my Grandmother, this aunt crisply
replied: "Of course I remember him. When he was the
Rector in Rockville, Maryland, some people went to my
father, and asked why he did not go call on his first cousin,
the Rev. Arthur S. Johns. Father replied: 'If he has anything to see me about he knows where I am.' Neither of
those first cousins ever spoke to the other."

Yes, my Grandmother and some of her older daughters
had told me that Henrietta Johns South Byrne and Bishop John
Johns were sister and brother, and that the wealthy father
of Henrietta Johns disowned his daughter because she, at
Upperville, Virginia, on Nov. 13, 1823, married James Byrne,
Jr., an Irishman, who then was living on the Pursley, Priestly
or Prestley farm. (In 1866 it took one day to travel by
stagecoach the fifty-two miles from Alexandria to Paris,
Virginia.) The name of Henrietta's father was never men-
tioned in the Byrne family, nor were her parents' names ever
recorded in a Byrne Bible. It also is possible that Kensey
Johns did not approve of Henrietta's first husband, Thomas
South, whom she married at Alexandria, Virginia, but I have
no knowledge as to whether Kensey Johns approved of
Thomas South. Thomas South owned no slaves in 1819.
Kensey Johns owned two slaves in 1800 and none by 1810.

At no place in the *History of the Theological Seminary In
Virginia* do I find the slightest reference to the name of Bishop
John Johns' father, the Chief Justice and afterwards Chan-

161

cellor of Delaware. But why? Why all the stone-silence about
Bishop Johns' family background?

Bishop Johns was Rector of Christ Church, in
Baltimore, when according to the Byrne Bible, Henrietta
died, in Upperville or near Paris, Virginia, on Sept. 1, 1837,
"in the full and confident hope of resurrection to Eternal
life." All that my Grandparents knew about the conduct of
Kensey Johns, III, they had learned from Henrietta's
second husband, James Byrne, Jr. (1797-1863), and from
Henrietta's oldest child, Catherine D. South, who brought
up John William Byrne, and he retained a lifelong recollec-
tion of his mother's smile, her pretty blue eyes and of how
sweet and kind she was to him. This son deeply loved his
mother, and equally as deeply resented her having become an
outcast from her Johns family.

The disowning and banishing of Henrietta is of no importance, except (1) possibly to cast light on why Dr. McKim,
in his biographical essay on Bishop Johns, omitted the name
of Bishop Johns' father, and (2) possibly to explain why the
Rev. John Johns and his far less robust brother, the Rev.
Henry Van Dyke Johns, never returned as a Rector to a
church in Delaware. Delaware had no Bishop until 1841 but
there were Episcopal Churches in Delaware. These unpleasant realities emphasize, and make crystal clear, that Bishop
Johns did not build his blameless life on his prominent and
aristocratic connections in Delaware.

Dr. McKim began his biographical essay with these pointed
words: "We are seriously embarrassed by the fact that no life
of this eloquent and distinguished prelate has ever been published. . . ." Dr. McKim, who personally had known Bishop
Johns for years, and knew the name of Bishop Johns' father,
relates: "As to his churchmanship, he (Bishop John Johns)
was unwaveringly attached to the Church of his birth. His
father, a communicant and Warden of the Episcopal Church
in New Castle, Delaware, was thoroughly loyal to the Prayer

Book. . . ." The name of that father is conspicuously not mentioned but Dr. McKim did have full knowledge of the Bishop's father's name.

Of couse Dr. McKim was right, because, for one year (1802), Chief Justice Kensey Johns, III, (1759-1848), was Warden of Immanuel Church, New Castle, Delaware. On February 9, 1959, in reply to my letter to the Rector of Immanuel Church, a distinguished spokesman for that Church wrote that "our records are not entirely complete and there are *gaps of certain years,* yet so far as I can ascertain Kensey Johns was a vestryman continuously from 1786 to 1842 . . . a short biography of Chancellor Johns (both Senior and Junior) was written by my grandfather, George B. Rodney, in *1 Delaware Chancery Reports, 490* . . . my family has lived adjoining the house of Chancellor Johns since 1830 and I was born (1882) in the adjoining house built by Kensey Johns, Jr. (1791-1857) . . . Kensey Johns (1759-1848) married Ann Van Dyke, on April 30, 1784, in the house we now call Amstel House, the home of the New Castle Historical Society. . . ." Was Henrietta merely dropped into one of those "gaps of certain years"?

Geo. B. Rodney was one of the attesting witnesses to the will of Kensey Johns, III, (1759-1848). In *30 Federal Cases, 1150,* there is an interesting account of the arbitration of the New Jersey—Delaware boundary dispute, at which Chancellor Kensey Johns, III (1759-1848), though eighty-eight years of age, appeared as a witness before John Sergeant, Esquire. Based on the Church Records, writes Judge Rodney, Chief Justice "Kensey Johns seems to have been baptized, on August 27, 1815," at age 56. Kensey Johns, III, who read law with George Read, one of the "Signers," came to Delaware about 1780, from Sudley, at West River, Maryland, and at age twenty-five married Ann Van Dyke, age fifteen. Thus were united two of the most influential families of Delaware and Maryland.

When Dr. McKim was writing his biographical essay on

Bishop Johns, about 1816, there was available to Dr. McKim a considerable amount of personal knowledge and published data on the Kensey Johns family of Delaware. Let me put my finger on some of that biographical data.

To begin with, Dr. McKim may have written to Immanuel Church, New Castle, Delaware, and learned that its records were "not entirely complete." One early biography ominously avoids Henrietta by these words: "Known Children." Dr. McKim also knew that John Johns was graduated from Princeton in 1815, so he must have known that Princeton had the records of deceased alumni. At last I was on the trail of Henrietta's father.

Princeton advised me as follows: "Our records on Bishop John Johns state that he was the son of Kensey Johns, Chancellor of Delaware, and Ann Van Dyke, daughter of Governor Nicholas Van Dyke, of Delaware. Kensey Johns, a lawyer, born in West River, Maryland, June 14, 1759, was married (April 30) 1784, and died in New Castle, Delaware, December 21, 1848. Ann Van Dyke was born August 9, 1768, and died October 21, 1839.

"John Johns was born in New Castle, Delaware, July 10, 1796.

"Married (1) Julianna E. W. Johnson, daughter of Col. Baker Johnson, Frederick, Maryland, November 20, 1820. Issue: Julianna, b. Jan. 3, 1822; Catharine Ross, b. Oct. 4, 1823; Kensey, b. Sept. 1, 1825, d. 1909; John Henry, died in infancy; Ann Van Dyke, b. Sept. 25, 1829, and John." (Julianna Johnson Johns died prior to 1836.)

"Married (2) Margaretta Jane Shaaff of Georgetown, D. C., daughter of Dr. John T. Shaaff, 1842." (According to the Baltimore *American* this marriage took place on July 17, 1838.) "Issue: Arthur Shaaff, b. Oct. 10, 1843.

"Married (3) Mrs. Southgate (maiden name Dixon), 1856. No issue." Mrs. Southgate's maiden name may have been Taylor, of Norfolk, Virginia.

CHIEF JUSTICE KENSEY JOHNS, III
Father of Bishop Johns

Courtesy of the Frick Museum and Delaware State Archives

164a

Last Will & Testament of John Johns of Fairfax County Virginia.

The pictures of my father, & mother & myself I give & devise to my son John Johns.

My gold watch I give to my grandson John Johns 1st.

To my faithful Servant Albert, I give one hundred dollars.

To my granddaughter Jane S Peyton I give One Hundred & fifty dollars in U. States 5 20.

I appoint my sons. Kensey Johns, John Johns & Arthur S Johns, the executors of this my last will & testament.

I leave no debts. Any money to my credit in the First National Bank, Alexandria — or in the Chesapeake Bank, Baltimore, or due as salary or otherwise I will to be used for paying my funeral expenses — & expenses wh. may be incurred in settling my estate — If there is a surplus I give & devise it to my daughter Juliana, whom I hereby appoint & constitute my residuary legatee.

John Johns
Malvern May 29. 1872.

Holographic Will of Bishop John Johns

164b

"Bishop Johns graduated from Princeton in 1815 and during his student days roomed with his classmate, Dr. Charles Hodge. Attended Princeton Theological Seminary, 1816-1819. . . .

"Our records state that Governor Nicholas Van Dyke, father of Ann Van Dyke Johns, was born September 25, 1738. He was President of Delaware, 1783-1786; Governor of Delaware, 1783-1789. He died at St. George's Hundred, February 19, 1789." Note: Delaware Governors, first called Presidents, were not elected by the people until 1792.

Bishop Johns is known to have been in Alexandria, Virginia, as early as 1824, and according to the records in two Byrne Bibles lying here before me, his sister, Henrietta Johns, prior to 1823, had married Thomas South, at Alexandria, Virginia. Vol. 39, p. 3, of Land and Personal Property Tax Assessments, proves that in 1819, Thomas South was living on Prince Street, Alexandria, Virginia. Brother Henry V. D. Johns was in Alexandria, Virginia, by 1831; their nephew, Kensey Johns Stewart, was in Alexandria by 1836, and their cousin Leonard Hollyday Johns was in Alexandria, Virginia, between 1823 and 1826.

J. Hall Pleasants, in his notes in Md. Historical Society Sheets, Nos. 165, 166, 167, 172, wrote that the painting of Kensey Johns, III, probably was done by J. R. Lambdin (H. Mathewson), monogram "R. L. 1840"; that the painting of Ann Van Dyke (Mrs. Kensey Johns, III), was done by Miss Sarah M. Peale; that the painting of Captain Kensey Johns, II, of Maryland, born, Mar. 11, 1721, died May 26, 1763, the son of Kensey Johns, I (1689-1729) of Calvert County, Md., and the father of Kensey Johns, III (1759-1848) probably was done by John Wollaston. Kensey Johns, II, married Nov. 15, 1749, Susannah Galloway (born about 1728), daughter of Richard Galloway (1702-1732) of London, and of Anne Arundel County, Md., and his wife, Mary Paca, aunt of the "Signer." Kensey Johns, II, was High Sheriff of Anne Arundel County, Md. See: F.A.R.L. No. 4528. Dr. Pleasants also wrote of the painting, probably by John Wollaston, of Susannah Galloway (Mrs. Kensey Johns, II). She was living in 1790. See F.A.R.L. No. 4530.

Kensey Johns I (1689-1729) was the son of Richard Johns (1649-1717), a Quaker who emigrated to Maryland prior to 1672, settled at "The Cliffs," in Calvert County in 1675, and in 1676, married Elizabeth Kensey, widow of Thomas Sparrow.

The four above described portraits, in 1920, were owned by Mrs. Bruce Cotten, "Clyburn," Green Spring Avenue, Baltimore, Maryland. Her husband, Major Cotten, presented those four portraits to the State of Delaware, and those paintings, and the one of Kensey Johns, IV (1791-1857), by C. W. Schreyler, the orginal of which hangs in the Court of Chancery, Wilmington, Delaware, appear in this biography, because of the generous cooperation of Leon de Valinger, Jr., Archivist, State of Delaware; also the Frick Art Reference Library, and the Maryland Historical Society helped me locate and obtain these family background illustrations.

The Rev. Dr. Henry Van Dyke and Lavinia (Montgomery) Johns had Henry Van Dyke Johns, II, born in Baltimore, Maryland, October 22, 1832, died September 11, 1897, married January 3, 1867, Annie E., the daughter of Col. George and Mary J. (Perkins) Davis, whose daughter Edyth Johns married, first Jesse Tyson, second Bruce Cotten.

Dr. Packard wrote that "Bishop Johns inherited "Sudley" through his father from an uncle, Captain John Johns, and he often spent part of his summers there . . . the place is now (1902) owned by his son, Dr. Kensey Johns of Norfolk, of the fifth generation. . . ." Dr. Kensey Johns died in 1909, and was buried at "Sudley." Actually Bishop Johns willed two hundred acres of this estate to his son, the Rev. Dr. Arthur S. Johns, and the remainder of "Sudley" to his son, Dr. Kensey Johns (1825-1909).

Cornelia Johns Grice, who had inherited the old house and most of the land of Sudley from her father, Dr. Kensey Johns, deeded it to Mr. and Mrs. William F. Kelly.

In *Sketches of Early Ecclesiastical Affairs in New Castle, Delaware, and History of Immanuel Church,* by Thomas Holcomb, published in 1890, Dr. McKim could have found a copy of a tombstone inscription reading:

"In memory of Kensey Johns, Chief Justice and afterwards Chancellor of the State of Delaware. Born: June 14, 1759, died December 21, 1848 . . ."

The above cited *History of Immanuel Church,* at pp. 200, 204, 206 and 207, states that Fidelia Johns, daughter of Kensey and Ann, (born, January 18, 1785, died February 20, 1871) was baptized March 27, 1785 (she married Major Thomas Stockton, who became Governor of Delaware in 1844); that son Kensey, Jr. (born Dec. 10, 1791, d. March 28, 1857) (ancestor of the Rev. Kensey Johns Hammond) was baptized September 8, 1792; that son John (Bishop John Johns, born July 10, 1796) was baptized October 13, 1796, at the age of three months, and that son Van Dyke Johns (born Nov. 15, 1798, died Feb. 15, 1801) was baptized August 25, 1799, at the age of eight months. We know that the above church records contain ominous "gaps of certain years," and do not name all seven of Kensey Johns' children who were living in 1816. And why do I make that assertion?

Lying here before me are photostatic copies of Kensey Johns' will of 1839 (executed two years after the death of his daughter, Henrietta, in 1837), with codicils of 1844 and 1848, probated December 25, 1848. Therein Kensey Johns (1759-1848) of sound mind and memory, named his sons: Kensey, Henry Van Dyke (born Oct. 23, 1803, died April 22, 1859, at Baltimore, Maryland) and John, and his daughters: Fidelia Stockton, Susannah Stewart (born December 16, 1789, died, December 6, 1862, m. January 2, 1812, Dr.

David Stewart, parents of Dr. McKim's friend for over forty years, the Rev. Dr. Kensey Johns Stewart, who died in Richmond, Virginia, June 10, 1902, aged 86 years), and Miss Ann Johns (born, Sept. 10, 1787 and died Sept. 23, 1874), a maiden lady who lived all of her life in the house her father had built in New Castle, Delaware. But daughters Henrietta Johns, Susanna Johns (1789-1862), and Ann Johns (1787-1874), and son Henry Van Dyke Johns (1803-1859) are not mentioned in the *History of Immanuel Church*. We also know that some of the seven Johns children were Presbyterians in 1816. Unfortunately the records of the Presbyterian Church of New Castle, Delaware, "founded in 1657," were burnt in 1800.

To repeat: neither Bishop Johns (who said he was the fifth child in his family) nor the Rev. Dr. Henry Van Dyke Johns ever became a rector of any church in Delaware, yet Vestryman Kensey Johns, III, was able to have his son, U. S. Congressman Kensey Johns, IV, appointed to the new office of Chancellor, created in 1832, by the new Constitution of Delaware. The father, after about thirty years as Chief Justice of Delaware, resigned in 1830 to become Chancellor, presumably to hold that office until 1832, for his son, Congressman Kensey Johns, Jr. Kensey, Sr. and Jr. held the positions of Chief Justice and Chancellor for fifty years. Dr. E. L. Goodwin wrote that Kensey Johns, "probably the father, was a lay delegate from Delaware to at least one of the earlier General Conventions" of the Episcopal Church.

Miss Elizabeth Booth, in 1875, at the request of her family wrote some notes which were published for the family in 1884 under the title *Reminiscences of New Castle, Del.* At page 79, in speaking of some action of hers in 1816, she says:

"It was about this time that Mr. John Johns, now Bishop of Virginia, then studying for the ministry, a young man of warm devoted piety, returned home from the seminary at

Princeton and conducted weekly meetings for prayer and exhortation in private houses. They were well attended. Many Christian hearts rejoiced and of those who had been indifferent many were brought to attend to their eternal interests. These zealous efforts promised well for the future ministry of Mr. Johns and that promise was abundantly realized in his usefulness and the success of his labors in after life."

Miss Booth, writing in 1875, makes no mention of ever again seeing Bishop Johns in New Castle, Delaware, after 1816. But, wrote Dr. Packard, Bishop Johns "often spent part of his summers" at "Sudley," West River, Maryland.

Dr. McKim was "seriously embarrassed," so he discreetly refrained from mentioning the name of Bishop Johns' father and thus had to omit the whole family background. Dr. McKim wrote that "the best account that the writer of this sketch has been able to find is that given by the Reverend Dr. Joseph Packard (1812-1902) in his *Recollections of a Long Life,* published in 1902, by his son, the Reverend Dr. Thomas J. Packard, who died 1912, at Rockville, Maryland, and who had followed Bishop Johns' son, the Rev. Dr. Arthur Shaaff Johns, as Rector of Christ Episcopal Church, Rockville, Maryland. Dr. McKim had read Dr. Packard's *Recollections of a Long Life,* so Dr. McKim knew the name of Bishop Johns father. On December 27, 1815, Kensey Johns IV was elected Clerk of the Session of the Presbyterian Church. On August 27, 1815, Kensey Johns III, at age 56, was baptized in the Episcopal Church.

Men of the Church, who for many years had associated with Bishop Johns, knew almost nothing of the Bishop's life in Delaware. Dr. E. L. Goodwin writes: "Of the Bishop's boyhood we know little." Bishop Johns said, "I was raised in the Episcopal Church, and I entered her ministry because of my training and my preference, and because I was convinced that it had the only form of Church government revealed in the New Testament."

Dr. Packard "heard him say that from the time of his parents' death there had never been one day that he had not brought them before his mind as they looked when he saw them last." Bishop Johns simply did not refer to his boyhood days, or to his father by name, or title.

About 1816 Dr. Charles Hodge, a Princeton classmate, went home with John Johns, and related that "In Chief Justice Johns' family some of the children were (baptized) Presbyterians and others (baptized) Episcopalians." Henrietta, one of the seven children living in 1816, was then about sixteen years old.

The full story of why Kensey Johns disowned and banished his daughter, Henrietta, will not be known until, as the Arabs say, "the stars grow old, the sun grows cold, and the leaves of the judgment book unfold."

Kensey Johns' Bible printed in Ireland—1793

The Kensey Johns family record in the Kensey Johns Bible, printed in Ireland in 1793, obviously was copied after 1793 and before 1839, from a prior family Bible but with marriage records omitted. Some early biographies read "known children" and omit Henrietta. The Bible of 1793 ominously designates Susannah as the "third daughter." Yes, and she also was the third child. The records of Immanuel Church "are not entirely complete and there are gaps of certain years," and Kensey Johns, III (1759-1848), although a Vestryman of that Church continuously from 1786 to 1842, was not baptized until August 27, 1815. In 1810 there were four daughters in the Kensey and Ann (Van Dyke) Johns family, but Henrietta, b. about 1800, d. 1837, was disowned and banished from her family by her proud father. She is a child left out of the family records in the above 1793 Bible.

Possibly Kensey Johns had other reasons for obtaining a new family Bible, that is, the one printed in Ireland in 1793, because in 1800, this gentleman apparently had two sons and one daughter by a wife other than Ann (Van Dyke) Johns. These two sons and one daughter, presumably the children of Kensey Johns, III, were born prior to his marriage, on April 30, 1784, to Ann Van Dyke. Their eldest daughter, Fidelia, was born a few days less than nine months after the marriage, to-wit: Fidelia was born Jan. 18, 1785; therefore, the two sons and one daughter enumerated in the 1800 Census (Vol. One, p. 207) and born prior to 1785 could not have been the children of Kensey Johns' second wife, Ann Van Dyke. The three remaining daughters, Ann, b. 1787, who never married; Susannah, b. 1789, m. 1812, and Henrietta b. about 1800, plus their mother total the four females established and enumerated in the 1810 Census, for New Castle, Delaware.

Ann (Van Dyke) Johns was 15 years old (b. Aug. 9, 1768) at the time of her marriage to Kensey Johns III, and their children were born in 1785; 1787; 1791; 1796; 1798; about 1800 (for Henrietta), and 1803.

With the family data established beyond any doubt, it is understandable that the biography of Kensey Johns appearing in *1 Delaware Chancery, 490,* is silent as to his children. Dr. McKim chose to use the words "seriously embarrassed" in his biographical essay on Bishop Johns. Henrietta Johns South Byrne, b. about 1800, d. 1837, had told the story of her banishment to her second husband, James Byrne, Jr. (1797-1863) and to her daughter, Catherine (South) Spalden, who brought up my grandfather, and he hated the whole Johns tribe, because of the way his mother had been treated by her father. John William Byrne and the Rev. Arthur Shaaff Johns, though first cousins, refused to speak to one another.

The luck of the Irish was with me, even though it took me two years to find corroborating evidence in support of Henrietta's own account; and one hundred and fifty years for the truth crashed to earth in the days of her youth to

come to light on microfilm in the National Archives: Chief
Justice Kensey Johns III, may his soul rest in peace, has, at
long last, been caught in the crossfire of the 1800 and 1810
Censuses, for New Castle Hundred, Delaware. Vol. One, p.
177.

The U. S. Census of 1810: Fidelia, the eldest of the four
daughters, prior to 1810, had married Thomas Stockton, so
they, and their baby, are listed together in the U. S. Census
of 1810; therefore, the three remaining daughters, Ann,
Susannah and Henrietta, plus their mother, totaled the four
females established by the 1810 U. S. Census, for New
Castle, Delaware. Add sons: Kensey, John and Henry V. D.,
and one has the seven children mentioned by Dr. Packard.

There are many tenderly restored churches in Virginia but
nowhere in America can one find such an architectural gem of
devotion and inspiration as is the new Trinity Episcopal
Church of Upperville, Virginia. Within a hundred and fifty
feet of its front door is the rectory where, in October of 1960,
I found its dedicated Rector, the Reverend Robert E. Cox,
living with his elderly mother. From our previous letters Mr.
Cox knew I was there in search of some word on Henrietta
Johns, so he took me to the historian of Upperville, Mrs.
Marie B. Gibson, who knows in intimate detail the story of almost every farm, of every old family and, together with her
husband, is related to many of the native Virginia families
of the old Leeds, and newer Meade, Parishes of Virginia.

Almost before I had finished relating the story of Henrietta's banishment, Mrs. Gibson interrupted with vim and
vigor—of course she knew, her great-aunt had told her that
Henrietta Johns South Byrne had been disowned by her
wealthy father from some place out of Virginia, because
Henrietta had married the Irish overseer of a farm between
Upperville and Paris, Virginia. Mrs. Gibson did not mention
the name, Henrietta, but she did know from the lips of her

mother, now 88, and from her great-aunt,* that this happened over a hundred years ago to a lady who married a Byrne, who lived near Upperville, Virginia. Moreover, Mrs. B. Curtis Chappelear, aged 74 in 1960, also told us that as a young girl she too had been told this same story by elderly ladies there in the Upperville area of the Blue Ridge Mountains of Virginia. Note: Chief Justice Johns owned no slaves in 1810, and no doubt abhorred slavery.

Gossip? Yes, and shocking too—remembered because it was so rare and revolting. One little tender-hearted girl (my Mother) felt so sorry she would cry when her father told of how cruelly his Mother, Henrietta Johns South Byrne, had been treated by her own father. Henrietta Johns, the granddaughter of Governor Nicholas Van Dyke of Delaware, died "in the full and confident hope of resurrection to Eternal life."

Johns v. *Herbert, 2 Appeals Cases D. C. 485-1894,* tells us that Bishop Johns, of Fairfax County, Virginia, died April 5, 1876, and left a will, dated: May 29, 1872, which was duly probated in Fairfax County, Virginia. The will originally bequeathed Chesapeake and Ohio Canal bonds of 1844, face value $6,000.00, to Bishop Johns' son, John Johns, Esquire (1831-1894), then of Richmond, Virginia, but later, by codicil, dated: April 1, 1876, Bishop Johns changed this gift from son John, to Mary McGuire Johns (1831-1918), daughter of the Rev. John P. McGuire and wife of son John, in trust, for her life, remainder to the children of John and Mary Johns, namely, John Johns, Jr. (1864-1922), Arthur Johns (1871-1936), and Maria Mercer Johns (1870-1938), who married Julian McShane and had Arthur Johns McShane, b. 1904, the only known descendant, in 1960, of Bishop Johns. Arthur Herbert and Cassius F. Lee were named executors. Lee did not act as Trustee. Herbert pretended that the

---

* Elizabeth Ann Robinson (1835-1926), whose mother was Agnes Fletcher Robinson, b. 1805, d. 1895.

bonds were good but rushed to sell his own bonds, retaining the Johns Trust bonds until they became worthless. Colonel Herbert, a bond broker, as Trustee, had to account for the loss occasioned by his apparent breach of trust.

Cassius F. Lee, Esquire, was Treasurer of the Board of Trustees of the Theological Seminary In Virginia from 1865 to 1890, and Colonel Arthur Herbert, Sr., was Treasurer of the Board from 1890 to 1911.

Mrs. Hite wrote in *My Rappahannock Story Book* that cut on a window-pane in the parlor at "The Shade," built in 1780 and one of Rappahannock's most beautiful homes, "is . . . 'Helen Lane 1866,' she the belle of 'Rose Hill' . . . home of William Armistead Lane and his wife Eliza Green . . . There was at 'Rose Hill' a garden, and in the garden was rare old English boxwood, slips of which were planted in the 'Ellerslie' garden . . . In 1926 the wonderful old box-wood, that had been growing in the 'Ellerslie' garden since 1815, was removed to the 'Bishop's Garden' at the National Cathedral in Washington (D. C.) . . . Helen Lane, grand-daughter of Eliza Green Lane, who first cared for the box-wood . . . came to the (Bishop's) garden to see the box-wood from the home of her girlhood. She was the wife of Rev. Arthur Johns, son of Bishop Johns, and the beauty and belle of 'Rose Hill' in the seventies."

The Rev. Dr. Arthur Shaaff Johns, D.D., was graduated from the Episcopal Seminary In Virginia, in 1873, and died in 1921. A few years prior to 1939, Mrs. Helen Lane Johns was living with her oldest child, Rosalie Van Dyke Johns, at 3215 Adams Mill Road, N.W., Washington, D. C.

BIBLIOGRAPHY

Note: Partial List

Bassett, J. S., *The Life of Andrew Jackson,* Macmillan, 1928

Beveridge, A. J., *The Life of John Marshall,* Houghton Mifflin, 1916

Boykin, B. A., *A Treasury of Southern Folklore,* Crown, 1940

Bradford, G., *Lee The American,* Houghton Mifflin, 1912

Brydon, G. MacLaren, *Highlights Along the Road of the Anglican Church*

Channing, Edward. *A. History of The United States,* Macmillan Co., 1919-1926

Delaplaine, Edward S., *The Life of Thomas Johnson,* Hitchcock, 1927

Delaplaine, Edward S., *Francis Scott Key,* Biography Press, 1937

Fiske, John, *Old Virginia and Her Neighbours,* Houghton Mifflin, 1897

Freeman, Douglas S., *Lee's Lieutenants,* Scribner's Sons, 1945

Goodwin, Wm. A. R., *History of The Theological Seminary in Virginia,* DuBois, 1923-24

Helfenstein, Ernest, *History of All Saints' Parish,* Marken & Bielfeld, 1932

Johns, John, *A Memoir of the Life of the Right Rev. William Meade, D.D.,* Innes & Co., 1867

Leake, W. E. H., *The American Revolution,* Appleton, 1898

Leftwich, the Rev. Dr. William Madison *Martyrdom In Missouri,* 1870

Lodge, H. C., *The Story of the Revolution,* Scribner, 1903

Maurice, F., *Robert E. Lee The Soldier,* Houghton Mifflin, 1925

McGuire, Mrs. Judith W., *Diary of a Southern Refugee*

Moore, J. Staunton, *History Henrico Parish and Old St. John's Church,* Williams Printing Co., 1904

Meade, Bishop, *Old Churches, Ministers and Families of Virginia,* Lippincott Co., 1857

175

Morison, Samuel Eliot, *American Revolution,* Clarendon, 1923

Muzzey, D. S., *A History of Our Country,* Ginn & Co., 1955

Packard, Joseph, D. D., *Recollections of a Long Life,* Byron
    S. Adams, 1902

Shea, J. G., *The Story of a Great Nation,* N. Y. Pub. Co.,
    1886

Thwaites, R. G., *The Colonies,* Longmans, Green & Co., 1926

Walker, Williston, *A History of the Christian Church,*
    Scribner's Sons, 1929

Wilson, Woodrow, *George Washington,* Harper & Bros.,
    1896

Wilson, Woodrow, *A History of the American People,* Har-
    per & Bros., 1902

Wilson, Woodrow, *Division and Reunion,* Longmans, 1921

Wood, John Sumner, *Cupid's Path In Ancient Plymouth,* Judd
    & Detweiler, 1959

Wood, John Sumner, *American History You Should Know*
    (Unpublished)

Wood, John Sumner, *Malta: Its International and Christian
    Aspects,* B. S. Adams, 1935

Wood, John Sumner, *Laws Everyone Should Know* in *The
    American Citizens Handbook,* The National Education
    Association, 1941

INDEX

Abert, Bache, 113
Acquia Creek, 61
Adam's Equity, 105
Adams, Mrs. John Quincy, 22
Adams, Samuel, 124, 125
Alabama, Bishop of, 52
Alexander, Dr. Archibald, 71
Alexandria Hospital, 30
Alexandria, Va., 38, 59, 61, 64, 113, 27, 141
All Saints' Church, Frederick, Md., 11, 13, 15, 16, 20
All Saints' Parish, 11, 17, 19, 22
Allen, Rev. Bennett, 14
"American Association," 125
American Colonization Society, 90
American Revolution (old), 15, 38, 82, 120
American Revolution causes, 124- 126
American Transportation, 138
Amissville, Va., 40, 43
Amstel House, 2, 163
Anaconda Plan, 35
Andros, Sir Edmund, 118
Angel, Peggy (dedication) v
Anglican Catholic Church of England, 14
Anglican Catholics, 32, 147
Annapolis, Maryland, 14, 125
Anne Arundel County, Maryland, 11
Anniversary, Semi-Centennial, 28
Apostolic Rite, 51
"Aristocrats" of Virginia, 135
Army of Northern Virginia, 23, 55
Army of the Rappahannock, 47
Articles of Religion, 72
Ashby, General, 40
Ashland Cottage, 47
Ashland Hall, 104
Ashland, Virginia, 44, 45, 47
Atkinson, Bishop, 58
Augusta, Georgia, 45, 52
Autobiography of William Lamb, 103, 109, 110
Bacon, Nathaniel, 31
Bacon, Rev. Thomas, 14

"Bacon's Laws of Maryland," 14
Baldwin, Dr., 87
Baltimore, Lord, 13, 19
Baltimore, Maryland, 15, 50, 56, 59, 139
Baptist Church of Amissville, 40
Baptists, 11, 32, 123, 124, 129
Barten, Rev. and Mrs., 39
Bassett, John S., 110
Battle of Bull Run, First, 35, 40, 42, 43
Battle of Manassas, the first, 43
Beall, William M., 13
Beauregard, General, 41
Ben Venue, 40
Berkeley, Royal Governor, 31
Beveridge, 115
Bibliography of Virginia, 87
Bishop of Alabama, 52
Bishop of London's Royal Commissary of the Established Church, 81
Bishop of Maryland, 4
Bishop of Massachusetts, 25
Bishop of New York, 56
Bishop of Oklahoma, 19
Bishop of Pennsylvania, 25
Bishop of Rhode Island, 15
Bishop of Southern Virginia, 107
Blair, Francis Preston, 35
Blair, Mrs. James, 119
Blair, Rev. Dr. James, 81, 82, 118
Bland, 83
"Bleeding Kansas," 3
Board of Trustees, 59, 68, 78, 91, 94, 95, 96, 98, 100
Board of Visitors, 85
Boat, 9
Booth, Elizabeth, 168
Boston, Mass., 63
"Boston Massacre," 125
Boston Tea Party, 125
Botkin, B. A., 129
Bowdoin College, 109
Bower, Rev., 15
Box cars, 45
Bracken, Rev. Dr., 85
"Briars, The," 40

Brodnax Resolution, 90
Brooke, Rev. Dr. John Thompson, 17, 19, 20
Brooke, Rev. Pendleton, 19
Brooke, Right Rev. Francis Key, 19
Brooks, Bishop Phillips, 147, 156
British Soldiers, 125
Brown, John, 33
Brown, Robert, 32
Browne, Bishop Harold, 69, 70
Browne, Peter, 33
Bryan, C. Braxton, 30, 96
Brydon, Rev. Dr. G. MacLaren, 8, 53, 55, 58, 60, 77, 81, 83, 84, 112, 158
Buggy, 9
Burke, 119
Burleigh, Stanhope, 106, 107
Burwell, Mr., 51
Byrd, Col., 119
Byrne, Henrietta Johns South, 2, 39, 161-173.
Byrne, James Jr., 161, 162, 171
Byrne, John William, 162, 171
Byrne, Octavia ("tender hearted girl,"), 173
Byrne, Sarah Ellen Dowden, 161
Calhoun, John C., 104
Calvert County, Maryland, 6, 12
Cambridge, Mass., 136
Camp and Navy Prayer Book, 49
Canterbury, 122
Capitol, Colonial, 32
Capitol of the Confederacy, 31
Carter's Hall, 51
Castleman, Rev., 96
Cathedral of Jesus, 7
Catholic Province of Quebec, 125
Catholics, 130
Centerville, Va., 43
Chancellor of Delaware, 158
Chandler, Dr. J. A. C., 88
Chandler, Vice Admiral Alvin Duke, 86
Channing, Professor, 33, 116, 139, 154
Chantilly, Va., 38, 39, 45
Chaplain to Lord Baltimore, 14
Charles Town, Md., 51
Charlottesville, Va., 142

Chesapeake and Ohio Canal Co., 139, 173
Chew, Samuel, 14
Chief Justice of Delaware, 16
Chief Justice of United States, 12
Christ Church, Alexandria, Va., 60, 63, 75
Christ Church, Baltimore, 19, 21, 22, 24
Christ Church, Charlottesville, 98
Christ Church, Navy Yard, Wash., D. C., 89, 113
Christ Church, Norfolk, Va., 104
Christ Church, Oxford, 139
Christ Church, Winchester, 93
Christian gentleman, 7
"Christian soldier, The," 122
Christ's family of Denominations, 5
Chrysostom, 61
Church Convention, 92, 94, 95
Church in the Confederate States, The, 112
Church of England, 32, 73
Church of the Presidents, 28
Church of Rome, 73
City Council, N.Y.C., 34
Civil War, 7, 9, 22, 29, 31, 33, 35, 36, 52, 59, 60, 87, 90, 111
Clay, Henry, 90, 104
"Cliffs, The," 6, 153
Coffee ($4.10 per lb.), 45
Cole, John, of Delaware, 59
College of William and Mary, 1, 78, 81, 82, 83, 84, 86, 87, 88, 91, 92, 93, 96, 97, 98, 99, 101, 104, 105, 106, 107, 108, 109, 111
Colonial aristocracy, 117
Colonial Churches in Virginia, 58, 87
Colonial Clergy, 115
Colonial Parish, 13, 14
Colonial Vestries in Virginia, 120
Colonial Virginia, 136
Colonial Williamsburg, Inc., 88
Colored people, 43
Colston, Mr., 96
Columbia, South Carolina, 6, 52, 127
Committees of Correspondence, 125
Compromises of 1820 and 1850, 140

Concord, Mass., 126
Confederate Army, 60, 128
Confederate Army Chaplain, 53
Confederate Bishop, 151
Confederate Generals, 45
Confederate gentlemen, 41, 42
Confederate Prayer Book, 53
Congregationalists, 123, 124
Constitutional Convention of 1787, 126
Consul to London, 22
Convert to the Episcopal Church, 14
Copton, Mr., 107
Corse, General, 52
"Cotton" Confederate Prayer Book, 52, 53
Council Journal, 57
Cox, Rev. Robert E., 172
Culpeper County, 40
Cummins, Bishop, 73
Curtis (or Curls) Neck, 102
Cushing, Jonathan Peter, 63
Custis, Daniel Parke, 118
Dame, Rev. Dr. William Meade, 61, 63
Dame, Rev. George Washington, 63
Danville, Virginia, 61
Dashiell, T. Grayson, 98, 102
Davis, Jefferson, 1, 32, 33
Davis, Mrs. Jefferson, 32, 33
Declaration of Independence, 82, 106
Declaratory Act, 124
Defender and Protector of the Church, 77, 112, 158
Defender of the Church, 8
Delaplaine, Judge Edward S., 20
Delaware, 7, 11, 16, 17, 21, 126, 129, 132
Delaware Chancery, one, 77, 172
Delaware Yankees, 77
Democratic Association, 104
Dew, Thomas Roderick, 85, 90, 103
Diary of a Southern Refugee 38, 150
Dickinson, John, 125
Dill, John, 18
Diocese of Virginia, 147, 155

Diocese of Washington, D. C., 65
Diocesan Missionary Society, 49, 55, 56, 91
Domestic Missionary Bishop, 5
Dudley, Bishop, 62
Dulany, Daniel, 14
Dulany, Lloyd, 14
Dulany, Patrick, 13
Dulany, Walter, 14
Dulles International Airport, 38
Early, General Jubal A., 51
Early railroad, 9
East All Saints' Street, 14
East-West National Pike, 11
Eastern Orthodox, 130
Eastburn, Dr., 25
Edge Hill, 89
Education Society, 28
Eliot, Charles William, 81
Elliott, Bishop, 52, 55, 58
Emmanuel Church, Baltimore, 22
Empie, Rev. Dr., 85
English Deism, 83
Episcopal Church in Africa, 64
Episcopal Church in America, 4
Episcopal Church in Brazil, 64
Episcopal Church in China, 64
Episcopal Church in Greece, 64
Episcopal Church in Japan, 64
Episcopal Church of New Castle, 72
Episcopal Church of Revolutionary Virginia, 78
Episcopal Church of Virginia, 84, 85, 98, 99, 100, 111
Episcopal Convention of Virginia, 138
Episcopal High School in Virginia, 152
Episcopal rectors, 4, 122
Erie Canal, 138
Established Church, 31
Established Church of England, 3
Established Church of Virginia, 122
Estate of John Johns, 78
Evangelical Knowledge Society, 57
Evangelical Revival, 5
Ewell, General, 48
Ewell, Prof. Benjamin Stoddert, 85, 86

Ewell, Pres. of Wm. & Mary, 81, 108, 109
Fairfax, Virginia, 38, 155
Farewell Address, George Washington, 3,
Federal Forces, 33, 51, 154
Federal retreat, 42
Federals, The, 40, 45, 53
"Fighter, The," 58
First Continental Congress, 125
First Episcopal Bishop of Virginia, 82, 131
First Lady of the South, 32
Fiske, John, 116, 118
Fitzhugh, George, 90
Flageolet, 63
Florida, 3, 40
Forest Hill, 40
Forsyth, Mary A., 29
"Forward to Richmond," 41
Franklin, Benjamin, 113, 121, 122
Frederick County, Maryland, 28
Ferderick Herald, 15
Frederick, Maryland, 4, 16, 19, 20, 21, 22, 50
Fredericksburg, Va., 45, 48
Frederick Town, Maryland, 11, 13, 16
Fredericktown, Maryland, 11, 28
Freeman, 154
French Revolution, 83, 136
Frick Art Reference Library, 166
Friend, Rev. Mr., 48, 49
Front Royal, Va., 40
Fugitive Slave Act, 127
Gage, General, 125
Gaines X Roads, 40
Gaithersburg, Maryland, 13
Galloway Plan, 125
Garlick, Col., 107
Garrett, Henrietta Byrne, 39
Garrison Forest, 15
Gatewood, Robert, 109
Gay Street, Baltimore, 19
Geiger, Henrietta, 27
General Convention in Baltimore, 69
General Conventions, 29, 56
General Council of the Church of the Confederated States, 52
General Theological Seminary, 21

"gentlefolk," 127, 136, 140, 144
George, III, King, 123
Georgetown, D. C., 13, 28, 143
German Lutheran, 11
German Reformed, 11
Gettysburg, Pa., 49
Gibson, Mrs. Marie B., 172
Gibson, Bishop, 9, 15, 37, 62
Goldsborough, William, 18
Good Friday, 46
Goodwin, Bishop Frederick D., 63
Goodwin, Rev. Dr. Edward L., 9, 15, 23, 43, 59, 77, 91, 103, 118
Governor of Maryland, First, 12, 21
Governor of Virginia, 86, 89
Grace Church, Alexandria, 75
Grace Church, Caroline County, 48
Grahame, John, 18
Grammar, Dr., 65
Grandy, Cyrus, 107
Great Planters, 34, 120
Green, Captain J. S., 39
Green, Col. John Shakelford, 40
Grenville, Prime Minister, 124
Grisby, Hugh Blair, 109
Griswold, 107
Grubhill Church, 110
Hagerstown, Maryland, 14, 15
Halifax County, Va., 44, 47, 51, 52
Halleck, Henry W., 155
Hamiltonian concept, 148
Hamilton's Crossing 47, 48
Hampden Sidney College, 63
Hancock government, 125
Hanover Junction (Doswell), 49
Hanson, John, 22
Harper's Ferry, 33 38
Harrison, Col., 83
Hartford Convention, 3
Harvard College, 62, 81, 82, 86, 109, 110, 111
Harvard Yard, 65
Hatch, Rev. Frederick W., 15, 16
Hayden, Rev. Horace Edwin, 60, 62, 65, 149
Hayes, President, 3, 140
"He Preached Unto Them Jesus," 132
Headly Vicars, 54

Heater, Robert, 140
Heath, General, 48
Hebrew, 59, 146
Helfenstein, Ernest, 16, 20, 21
Henry, Patrick, 33, 54, 121, 124, 135
Henshaw, Dr., 15
Herbert, Colonel Arthur, Sr., 63, 78, 174
"High Church," 24
High Sheriff of Anne Arundel Co., Md., 153
High Tariff, 34
Highlights Along the Road of the Anglican Church, 8, 58, 112
Hildreth, 119
"Hill, The," 6, 27, 63, 64, 67, 140, 146
History of All Saints Parish, 16
History of The Seminary in Virginia, 1, 30, 31, 61, 66
Historical Magazine of the Protestant Episcopal Church, 53, 112
Historiographer of the Diocese of Virginia, 8, 9, 15, 58, 77, 112
Hodge, Rev. Dr. Charles, 61, 78, 144, 165, 170
Hodges, Rev., 96
Holden Chapel, 110
Holland, 32
Holmes, Justice Oliver Wendell, 149, 150, 156
Holy Communion, the, 70
Holy Ministry, 6
Hopkins, Bishop John Henry, 73
Hopkins, Bishop of Vermont, 71
Hopkins, Johns, 153
Hopkins Hospital, Johns, 153
Hooker, the great, 73
"Horse and buggy Bishops," 141
Horseback, 9, 34
Hot Springs, Va., 47
House of Burgesses, 122
Hunter, Rev. Samuel, 14
Immanuel Church, New Castle, 163
Indians, 31
Intolerable Acts, 125
Jackson, Andrew, 110
Jackson, Thomas J. (Stonewall), 36, 41, 45, 48, 122, 154

Jacobs, Octavia Byrne Wood (dedication) v; 173
(Mrs. Judson Wriley Jacobs)
Jacobins, 82, 108
James River, 33, 154
Jay, 121
Jefferson, Thomas, 82, 83, 89, 119
Jenning's Ordinary, 110
Jennings, Rev. Joseph, 13
Jews, 123
Johns, Angelina E. Southgate, 38
Johns, Ann Van Dyke, 2, 77
Johns, Rev. Dr. Arthur Shaaff, 28, 29, 31, 39, 40, 65, 113, 155, 161, 169, 174
Johns vs. Herbert 2 App. D. C., 485, 173
Johns, Rev. Dr. Henry Van Dyke, 16, 21, 22, 28, 158, 159, 162
Johns, The Right Reverend Doctor John, 1, 2, 3, 4, 5, 7, 8, 9, 11, 12, 13, 15, 16, 19, 21, 22, 23, 25, 28, 29, 31, 38, 39, 40, 52, 54, 55, 56, 57, 58, 59, 60, 63, 64, 65, 66, 69, 70, 71, 72, 78, 79, 81, 159
Johns, Lieutenant John, 45
Johns, John Henry, 22
Johns, John, Jr., 54
Johns, John Lane, 40, 65
Johns, Helen Lane, 40, 174
Johns, Miss Julia, 30, 31, 54
Johns, Miss Julianna, 12, 17, 22, 155
Johns, Dr. Kensey (Major), 45, 98
Johns, Chancellor Kensey III, 153, 158, 167
Johns, Chancellor Kensey, LL.D., 158
Johns, Congressman Kensey III, 158, 168
Johns, Kensey, I, 153
Johns, Captain Kensey, II, 153
Johns, Chief Justice Kensey, III, 66, 98, 153, 158
Johns, Kensey, IV, 77, 158
Johns, Lavinia, 22
Johns, Rev. Leonard Hollyday, 27
Johns, Margaret (Shaaff), 102, 113
Johns, Mary Lavinia, 22
Johns, Richard, 6, 153

Johns, Rosalie Van Dyke, 39, 40, 174
Johns, Shaaff, 40
Johns, Col. Thomas, 27
Johns-McGuire cottage, 46, 47
Johns Hopkins Hospital,
Johnson, Colonel Baker, 12, 13, 17, 22
Johnson, Confederate General Bradley, 46
Johnson, Catharine Worthington, 17
Johnson, Joshua, 21
Johnson, General Thomas, 12, 21
Johnson, Thomas W., M.D., 22
Jones, Rev. A., 51, 96
Jones, Wm. Ellis, 98, 102
Kearny, General Philip, 44, 64
Keith, Dr., 89
Kemp, Bishop, 17, 24
Kensey, Elizabeth, 153
Kent, England, 73
Kentucky, 35
Key, Anne Phoebe Charlton, 20
Key, Francis Scott, 5, 11, 13, 20, 28, 143
King Cotton, 35
Kinsolving, Rev. Arthur B., D.D., 152
"Know-Nothing," 104, 108
Lafayette, General, 2
Lamb, William, 103, 104, 105, 106, 107, 108
Lamb's Autobiography, 87, 92
Lane, Helen, 40, 174
Latane, Rev. James A., 73
"Lawyer-Poet, the," 13, 28
Leaventhorpe, Col., 49
Lecky, 119, 120
Lee, Cassius F., 63, 174
Lee, Hannah, 53
Lee, Mrs. General, 38, 46
Lee, Richard Henry, 121
Lee, General Robert E., xiii, 1, 9, 23, 33, 36, 63, 64, 128, 150, 154
Lee's Episcopal Church, Lexington, Virginia, 23
Leesburg, Virginia, 37
Leftwich, The Rev. Dr. William Madison, 175

Letters of a Pennsylvania Farmer, 125
Lexington, Virginia, 23, 36
Libby Prison, 50
Liddon, Canon, 69, 70
Life of Bishop Meade, 157
Life of John Marshall, 115, 126
Lincoln, Abraham, 35
Lincoln pipe dream, 41
"Lion-hearted, the," 145, 147
Livingstons, 121
Locke, John, 82, 107
London, Bishop of, 135
London Dock, 107
London, England, 52, 53
Long Island, 34
"Lord, with Glowing Heart I'd Praise Thee," 5
Lord's Supper, 69, 70
"Low Church," 23, 25, 59
Lowell, Pres. of Harvard, iii
Loyalists, 121
Luther, Martin, 146
Madison, Bishop, 7, 81, 82, 83, 84, 131, 138
Madison, President James, 122, 138
Maine, 3
Main Liquor law, 106
"Malvern," 31, 38, 63, 64, 113, 155
Malvern Hill, Battle of, 154
Manassas, first, 40
Manassas Junction, 41, 122
Manhattan Island, 34
Mann, Rev., 96
Manuscripts, 132, 155
Marbury, Ogle, 62
Marshall, John, 3, 4, 83, 89, 137
Marye, Mr., 47
Maryland, 7, 11, 12, 23, 27, 35, 143
Maryland Bill of Rights, 14
Maryland Historical Society, 166
Maryland regiment, 49
Mason, 83
Massachusetts, 123
Mathews, Chailer, 130
Mayflower Compact, 33
Mayo, Peter P., 110
McClellan's Army, 155
McDowell, General, 41
McGill, Rev. J., 47

McGuire, Rev. E. C., 96
McGuire, Rev. Dr. John P., 44, 45, 46
McGuire, Mrs. Judith W., 38, 40, 43, 44, 45, 46, 150
McGuire, Mary Eleanore Mercer, 45
McIlvaine, Bishop, 73
McKim, Rev. Dr. Randolph H., 1, 60, 65, 66, 148, 162
McShane, Arthur Johns, 173
Meade, Hodijah, 110
Meade, Bishop, 5, 7, 15, 32, 39, 52, 54, 58, 59, 67, 71, 73, 77, 82, 84, 85, 92, 94, 95, 115-133, 137, 144, 145, 147, 148, 149, 156, 157, 158
Mecklenburg County, North Carolina, 82
Memoir of Bishop Meade, 67, 128, 157
Methodism, 3
Methodist, 11, 32, 129
Mexican War, 3, 140
Millwood, Virginia, 39, 51
Minie balls, 46
"Minutemen," 125
Missionary Bishop to Africa, 25
Missouri, 35
Monroe, James, 83, 122
Montgomery, Ala., 41, 52
Montgomery County, Maryland, 27, 63
Montgomery, Fidelia (Rogerson), 22
Montgomery, Lavinia, 22
Montgomery, Colonel William, 22
Monticello, 90
Monumental Church, 33, 137
Moody, Wm. M., 101
Moore, Bishop, 5, 7, 53, 77, 78, 83, 131, 132, 137
Moral Philosophy, 91
Morison, Samuel E., 139
Morrises, 121
Motley, 116
Mt. Vernon, Va., 65
"Mountain" Bishop of West Virginia, 22
"Mountain View," 35
Murphy, John, 107

"Mustard seed" of infidel France, 82
Nassau Hall, 128
National Road, 139
Navigation Act, 124, 125
Negroes, the, 6
Nelson, Mr., 96
Nelson, Colonel Hugh, 23
Nelson, John, 18
New Castle, Delaware, 2, 4, 22, 29, 31, 53, 98
New Hampshire, 63
"New Rebellion," 38
New Revolution, 127
Newton University, Baltimore, 27
New York City, N. Y., 34, 125
Nicholas, 83
Norfolk, Virginia, 31, 98
North Carolina Regiment, 49
North, Prime Minister Lord, 125
North-South Seneca Trail, 11
Northern Industrialists, 34
Northwest Territory, 125, 127
Norton, Dr., 89
Nottoway County, Va., 110
Nullification and Secession, 104
Ohio River, 37
Ohio Valley, 122, 141
Old Braddock Road, 13
Old Churches, Ministers and Families of Virginia, 78, 116, 120, 131
"Old Fuss and Feathers," 35, 42
Old Pohick Church, 64, 65
Old Revolution, 127
"On To Richmond," 41, 45
Ossawotomie, 33
Oxford Tracts, 71
Oxdrawn Wagon, 138
Packard, Dr. Joseph, 19, 59, 60, 65, 67, 69, 83, 89, 90, 109, 122, 139, 169
Page, Mr., 96
Page, Miss Betty, 108
Page, Miss Mattie, 108, 109
Paine, Tom, 105
Palmer, George Herbert, 62
Paris, Virginia (Byrne, James), 38, 161, 172
Parke, Daniel, 118
Parkersburg, 37

Parkman, Francis, 129
Parliament, 124
Parochial library, 18
Peachy, Professor, 91, 106
Peggy Stewart, 125
Pendleton, Rev. William Nelson (General), 23, 48
Pendletons, 83, 122
Penick, Dr., 24
Pennington, Dr., 55, 112
Perrin, 107
"Persons of Color," 19
"Periwig," 136
Peterkin, Bishop, 62
Peterkin, George, 22
Peterkin, Rev. Joshua, 22
Petersburg, Va., 49
Peyton, Henry, 30
Phenix Society, 106
Philadelphia, 19, 125
Phillips Brooks House, 136
Philomathean Society, 106, 108
"Pick-ups," 41
Pilgrims of Plymouth, 119
Pinckneys, 122
Pipe Creek Plantation, 20
Platt, Mrs. Fannie Amiss, 40
Point of Rocks, 37
Point Pleasant, 37
"Poor whites," 121, 129
Porcupine, Peter, 105
Port Walthall Junction, 52
"Potomac Seam," 140
Potomac River, 37, 38
Potter, Dr. Alonzo, 25
Potts, Richard, 18
Prayer Book, 52, 72
Presbyterians, 32, 36, 123, 124, 129
Prescott, Historian, 116
President of the Confederacy, 32, 52
Princeton, 4, 6, 17, 21, 82, 86, 111, 128, 132
Princeton Theological Seminary, 59, 78
Privileged State-Church, 14
Professor of Pastoral Theology and Homiletics, 70
Profiteering, Richmond, 47
Protector of the Church, 8

Protestant colonies, 125
Protestant Episcopal Church, 3, 5, 8, 15, 52
Protestant Reformation, 156
Protestant Reformation, Second, 15
"Public Virtue and Patriotism," 126
Quaker, 4, 124
Quaker ancestor, 6
Quantico, 61
Quebec Act, 125
Raleigh Parish, 110
Randolph, Alfred Magill, 107
Randolph, Bishop, 9
"Randolph" Confederate Prayer Book, 52, 53
Randolph, Richard, 96
Rappahannock County, Va., 36, 39, 43
Ravenswood, 37
Rawlings, Mary Leftwich, (dedication) v
Rebellion To Cleanse A Foul Union, 59
"Rebels," 150
Recollections of a Long Life, 67, 83, 87, 89
Reconstruction, 78
Rector in Maryland, 6
Rector of All Saints' Church, 23
Reformed Episcopal Church, 8
Reminiscences of a Long Life, 83
Republican Party of 1860, 127
Revolutionary War era, 115
Rhode Island, 82
Richmond, Virginia, 38, 39, 41, 43, 45, 46, 47, 52, 53, 54, 58, 60, 117, 153
"Riot of 1807," 129, 145
Robertson, 107
Rockbridge Artillery Company, 47
Rockville, Maryland, 113
Roman Catholic, 17, 20, 124
Roman Catholic Church, 11, 12, 147
Roman missionaries, 73
Ross, William, 18
Royal College of William and Mary, 81
Royal Colony, 31
Royal Governor, 118, 123
Rutgers College, 104

St. Andrews Church, Baltimore, Md., 21
St. James, Warrenton, Va., 43
St. John's Church, Wash., D. C., 28
St. Paul's Church, Alexandria, 54, 102
St. Paul's Church, Baltimore, 24
St. Paul's Church, Richmond, 5
St. Philip's Church, 43
St. Thomas' Church, 15
St. Thomas' Church, Orange, Va., 49
Salary, 18, 21, 55
Saunders, Mr., 107
Saunders, Professor, 85
Schley, D., Reg'r., 16
School of the Prophets, 59
Scot, Dred, 20
Scott, Union General Winfield, 36, 41, 42
Second Bishop of Virginia, 115, 131
Second Essay of Government, 82
Segar, Joe, 105
Seminary, at Alexandria, Va., 59, 60
Seminary Chapel, 68
Seminary Hill, 30, 31
Seminary in Virginia, 5
Seminary, the, 113
Seneca Indian trail, 13
Separation of Church and State, 111
Separatist Mayflower Pilgrims, 32
"Sermons on his mind," 17
Services, James A., 87, 114
Shaaff, Arthur, 12
Shaaff II, Arthur, 29
Shaaff, Captain Francis Key, 29
Shaaff, Dr. John Thomas, 28
Shaaff, Margaretta Jane, 28
Shaaff, Mary (Sydebotham), 28
Sheldon Hall, 108, 109
Shenandoah Valley, 56
Shepherdstown, Md., 51
Sheriff collecting tax of tobacco, 14
Signers of the Declaration of Independence, 123
"Simple folks," 121, 129, 138, 151
Smith, Rev. Aristides, 49

Smith, Dr. Augustine, 85
Smithsonian Institute, 64
Socialism, xiii
"Soldiers of the Cross," 61
Solomon's Sons, 108
"Sons of Liberty," 124, 125
South, Thomas, 161
South Carolina, 110
Southern Folklore, 129
Southern women, 33
Sparrow, Rev., 96, 131
Spartan simplicity, 6
Stamp Act, the, 124
Stamp Act Congress, 124
State of Virginia, 86
State Teachers' College, 86
Staunton (Virginia Convention at), 4, 143
Stealing Diaries, 40
Sterling, 121
Stewart, Rev. Dr. Kensey Johns, 60, 53, 65
Stone, Dr. W. M., 24
"Street Beggar in London, a," 14
Stuart, General J. E. B., 45, 52
Sudley, 153
Suffern, Thomas, Esq., 110
Sugar Act, The, 124
Sully, 107
Sumter, Fort, 34
Sunday School, 18, 29, 36
Swem, Dr. Earl G., 85, 87, 88, 90, 92, 103, 114
Taney, Roger Brooke, 11, 20
Taylor, Sarah, 40
Tea Act, 89, 125
Tea ($20.00 lb.), 45
The Virginia Bishop, 121, 129, 132, 133, 159
Theological Seminary at Alexandria, Virginia, 20, 114
Theological Seminary of Princeton, 4
Third Bishop of Virginia, 84
Thompson, Miss Julia, 108, 109
Tories, 121
Totten, Dr. Silas, 91, 102, 109
Townshend Duty Acts, 89, 124, 125
Townshend, Prime Minister, 124

"Tragic era" of Reconstruction 3, 127, 131
Trinity Church, D. C., 22
Trinity Church, Staunton, 75
Trotter, Dean, 30
Tucker, Bishop Beverley D., 60
Turretin, Swiss theologian, 69, 71
Tyler, John, 98, 100
Tyler, William B., 18
"Uncle Tom," 107
Union Army, 154, 155
Union soldiers, 33
Union, the, 34
Unitarian, 4, 32
University, State of New York, 6
Upper and Lower Brandon, 50
"Upper-class" Virginians, 5, 137
Upperville, Va. (Byrne, James), 38, 161, 172
de Valinger, Leon, Jr., 166
Van Dyke, Elizabeth (Nixon), 2
Van Dyke, Governor Nicholas, 2, 164, 165
Vestries of Virginia, 140
Vestry of All Saints, 13
Virginia, 7, 8, 23, 78, 126
Virginia Bishop, The, 2, 7, 8, 9, 129, 132, 133, 159
Virginia Churchman, The, 16, 23, 58, 77
Virginia Episcopal Church, 5, 7
Virginia Historical Index, 87
Virginia Regiment, 52d, 47, 48
Virginians, 5
Voice of Free Grace, The, 76
War Between Brothers, 61
War Between the States, the, 32, 59, 112
War of 1812, 3
War to Cleanse The Union, 3, 36, 127
War wrecked Parishes, 9
Warrenton, Virginia, 39
Washington, Bushrod, 90
Washington College, 150
Washington, D. C., 13, 22, 41, 42, 61, 113
Washington, General George, 2, 13 65, 83, 89, 104, 105
Washington, Martha, 118
Washington, Va., 43

Webster, Noah, 120
Wedemeyer, General Albert C., (Foreword) xi
West Point, 23
West River, Maryland, 77, 153
West Virginia, 146
Western Virginia, 35
Westover Manuscripts, 119
Wheeling, 37, 55
White, Bishop, 17, 21
White House, The, 27
Whittingham of Maryland, Bishop, 26, 53
Whittle, Bishop, 77, 131, 132, 147, 148
Williams, Bishop, 122
Williams, Margaret, 27
Williamsburg Society, 82
"Williamsburg: The Story of a Patriot," 88
Williamsburg, Virginia, 31, 81, 84, 85, 105, 113, 117, 126
Wilmer, Bishop Pere, 151
Wilmer, Rev. Richard Hooker, 52, 137, 151
Wilmer, the Rev. Dr. William Holland, 85, 137, 151
Wilmer, Dr. William Holland, 152, 153
Wilmer Eye Clinic, 153
Wilmington, N. C., 125
Wilson, Miss Janet, 110
Wilson, Woodrow, 117, 120, 154
Winchester, Rt. Rev. James A., 29
Winchester, Va., 51
Wirt, William, 104
Wolf, Simon, 89
"Wonderful Century, The," 138
Wood, Brooks Crosby Byrne (of Woodbyrne), xiii
Wood, Dr. David Eliab (Captain U.S.A. MC.), 114
Wood, John Sumner, xi
Wood, Mary Leftwich Rawlings (dedication), v
Wood, Mayor Fernando, 34
Wood, General, 83
Wood, Peggy Octavia, 114 v, 114
Wood, Peggy Angel (dedication),

Wood, Dr. Sumner, Jr. (Captain
U.S.A.F. MC.), 114
Woodis Hunter, 104
Woodville, Va., 43
World War 1, 13
Worthington, Miss Catherine, 12
Worthington, Col. Nicholas, 12
Wren Building, 87
Wren, Sir Christopher, 84
Writs of Assistance, 125

Wroth, Dr. Peregrine, 25
Wyatt, Rev. Dr. William E., 24,
25
Yankee, 127
Yankee Abolition Societies, 111
Yankee Bishop, 1, 29, 112
Yankee President (of Wm. & M.),
92
Yorktown Campaign, 83
Yorktown, Virginia, 23